CARE OF MIND
CARE OF SPIRIT

Care of MIND Care of SPIRIT

PSYCHIATRIC DIMENSIONS OF SPIRITUAL DIRECTION

Gerald G. May, M.D.

1817

HARPER & ROW, PUBLISHERS, SAN FRANCISCO

Cambridge, Hagerstown, New York, Philadelphia
London, Mexico City, São Paulo, Sydney

FIRST EDITION

Designer: Jim Mennick

Library of Congress Cataloging in Publication Data

May, Gerald G.
   CARE OF MIND/CARE OF SPIRIT.

   Bibliography: p. 169
   Includes index.
   1. Spiritual direction—Psychological aspects.
I. Title.
BV5053.M38   1982   253.5   81–47840
ISBN 0–06–065533–X   AACR2

82 83 84 85 86 10 9 8 7 6 5 4 3 2 1

To Tilden Edwards, who has guided me,
and to my patients in state hospitals and prisons
who will never hear of or benefit from formal spiritual guidance

Contents

Preface

The psychiatric dimensions of spiritual direction may seem small and insignificant when compared with the overwhelmingly essential movement of the Holy Spirit in people's lives. Yet these psychiatric phenomena are intimately related to the Spirit's movements and they deserve both attention and response.

I use the term *psychiatric* to denote a focus that is oriented towards pathology or disorder in contrast to other more general and descriptive behavioral sciences. Psychiatry is a medical specialty, the province of which is the diagnosis and treatment of mental disorders. Many other disciplines (including psychology, social work, counseling, and so on) may do much the same thing from a nonmedical standpoint. Most of what I have to say about psychiatry in the following pages can be applied to these other disciplines as well. I have chosen to focus on psychiatry, however, because it is the one field that attends specifically to matters of disorder (pathology) and cure. In contrast, spiritual guidance can hardly be called a disorder-focused discipline. It attends far more to growth, completion, and fulfillment than to correction of deficiency or illness. Yet historically it has been a part of the "cure of souls" and therefore must involve a caring for people's overall conditions. Clearly, this cannot be divorced from a caring for the healing of human minds. An informed "caring for" need not imply a manipulative "taking care of."

It has been my impression that the arena of psychopathology is seldom dealt with in a balanced way by spiritual directors: some tend towards excessive fascination while others try to avoid it entirely. I do not pretend to have perfected a balance in this work, but I do hope to contribute some steps in that direction. My expertise is in the field of psychiatry rather than theology, and this book should not be seen as a comprehensive introduction to spiritual direction itself. For those who desire such an introduction, I highly recommend Kenneth Leech's *Soul Friend* and Tilden Edwards's *Spiritual Friend* (see Bibliography).

My intention here is to provide a concise and practical discussion of a variety of psychiatric considerations encountered in spiritual direction. This means that we will often have to straddle the boundaries between theology and the behavioral sciences. I believe that these boundaries do exist, primarily because psychology as it has evolved in our culture does not—and perhaps cannot—really deal with the transcendent and divine realities of life. The people who practice the behavioral sciences certainly can deal with these realities in their own hearts, but the disciplines almost invariably fail to break free of their anthropocentric focus. It does no good, I think, to blur the boundaries that exist between theology and psychology, in the name of wholeness or integration. It is better to walk their rugged interfaces. I shall try to do this as clearly as possible in the discussions that follow.

It should be noted that, in order to ensure against any breach of confidence or privacy, all quotes and accounts relating to individual people in this work (except those attributed to specific authors or for which special permission has been obtained) are either composites based on typical responses or purely hypothetical. The themes are accurate, but the specific words and people portrayed are fictional. General references cited in footnotes will be found in the briefly annotated Bibliography at the end of the text. For this reason, publication data will not usually be included in the notes. The Bibliography is representative rather than complete, but I am quite certain it will be an adequate gateway into the wealth of literature pertaining to this area of study. Both Edwards and Leech provide many additional references. So does my soon-to-be-published work, *Will and Spirit: A Contemplative Psychology*, which lays out a comprehensive contemplative vision of human psychology and spiritual searching. Many areas that are briefly mentioned here are more fully dealt with in that book.

The Shalem Institute for Spiritual Formation (Mount St. Alban, Washington, D.C. 20016) has been my primary learning laboratory in this arena. I am deeply grateful for the enrichment I have been given as a participant and a leader in Shalem's programs. In

addition I wish to extend my appreciation to Fr. Tilden Edwards
(Shalem's Director), Rev. Mary Kraus, Rev. Lindsley Ludy, Fr.
Shaun McCarty, S.T., Sr. Rose Mary Dougherty, S.S.N.D., and
Dr. Roy Fairchild for their critical manuscript reviews, and to my
wife, Betty, who typed for me when my hands cramped and loved
me when my mind cramped. In addition I wish to thank Jessica
Morgan and the American Psychiatric Association for permission
to use material from *DSM-III.*

Finally, I wish to express my great indebtedness to those people
who have come to me over the years for psychological or spiritual
guidance or both. Their presence in my life and work has been my
richest education in grace.

1. Heritage: History, Definitions, and Distinctions

The essence of spiritual guidance or direction can be seen whenever one person helps another to see and respond to spiritual truth. It is a human relationship that seeks realization of that which is beyond human comprehension. Such relationships have existed in all times and places throughout history; some have been formal, some casual, some creative, and some destructive. The person of the spiritual guide has been called by many names: shaman, guru, mentor, rabbi, priest, pastor, mother, father, director, friend. The priests and wise men of ancient Judaism functioned as spiritual guides, though of course the Lord was clearly acknowledged as the "real" guide through the Law and Prophets. In Christianity, formal individual spiritual direction is usually seen as having begun in the third and fourth centuries, when many individuals sought guidance from desert hermits. Thereafter, the spread of monasticism had tremendous influence in refining and promulgating a variety of spiritual guidance traditions. It is somewhat difficult to trace the full history of this discipline in Christianity, primarily because there has been little consistency or consensus to its precise definition.[1] This vagueness still exists today.

There were times when individual spiritual direction was seen as a component of pastoral care and the cure of souls, or as intimately related to confession. At other times it has been felt to be a more distinct and separate discipline. At various points lay people have been encouraged and discouraged from acting as spiritual directors. Sometimes careful training was felt to be essential, but at other times there was more affirmation that the ability to guide souls could come as a graced gift or charism even in the absence of formal education. Formal spiritual direction has variously been identified as addressing the most intimate heart-journey possible for people (as in John of the Cross and Teresa of Avila), as relating primarily to matters of conscience and vocation (as in some developments that took place after the Council of Trent), as especially dealing with the discernment of good and evil spirits (as in Ignatius Loyola), or as involving psychological growth, individuation and self-actualization (as in some modern approaches).

Amidst changing forms and emphases, Roman Catholic, Anglican, and Orthodox traditions have maintained some ongoing structures for spiritual direction. For Protestants, however, there have often been special theological problems with the idea of one person advising another on intimate matters of the spirit. Much of the concern here has to do with sacerdotalism, the possibility that the methods or personality of the spiritual director would supplant the role of Jesus as the prime mediator between God and the individual human being. Thus Protestants have characteristically tended to rely more on group spiritual guidance in faith-sharing meetings and on the private experience of prayer and personal scriptural reflection.

Psychology's relationship to spiritual guidance has been especially interesting and dynamic. From the time of Christ until well after the Reformation, little differentiation was made between psychological and spiritual disorders. Many forms of insanity were seen as spiritual problems, caused by demonic possession or moral deficiency. This attitude continued basically unchanged into the nineteenth century. While medical science was developing physical explanations of organic disease, psychology remained bound to faith and morality. With the advent of Freudian psychoanalysis, however, drastic changes began to take place. Freud's idea was that the human mind could be studied scientifically through observation and measurement, and for many people this took psychology out of the realm of spirit.

Considering how long the old ideas had been maintained, the onslaught of modern psychology occurred with emphatic suddenness. Within a generation after Freud's work became known, psychotherapy was in many circles supplanting spiritual and moral guidance as the primary method of alleviating mental disorders. There ensued an age in which psychologists and psychiatrists were seen by many as a kind of "new priesthood."

People turned in great numbers to the new psychological theories for guidance on all kinds of matters: how to raise children, how to preserve marriages, how to achieve success, even how to find meaning in life. People still attended church, but for many—especially those in the so-called mainline churches—a schism had taken place. Church still offered fellowship, moral guidance, and a sense of rootedness in tradition, but it was often no longer the source of psychological and emotional guidance it had been for centuries. People still participated in the sacraments, but for some, rituals such as confession lost much of their felt transformations in reconciliation and atonement. Frequently it seemed that psychology promised more hope for wholeness, health, efficiency, and happiness.

In an attempt to keep up with the times, droves of clergy took psychological training. Many left parish churches to set up private practice in pastoral counseling or to teach others in clinical pastoral education. In such settings, the clergy were in a position of offering individual in-depth guidance to people, but in most cases this guidance became increasingly psychological and less and less spiritual. It is interesting to note that this movement towards counseling was almost entirely a Protestant venture. Relatively few Roman Catholic or Orthodox clergy entered these fields. I have often suspected that one of the reasons was that some traditions of formal spiritual guidance had been preserved in Catholicism and in the Eastern Church, while Protestants had little or none. For many Protestants, counseling offered the only available possibility for individual depth-helping. It must be acknowledged, however, that only a very small minority of Roman Catholics actually partook of individual spiritual direction, and much of that guidance was itself becoming increasingly psychological in nature or being limited to institutional models of dealing with sin and its remedies.

In the decade of the seventies another movement arose. A number of people had become disenchanted with traditional and even pop psychotherapies. Many had tried the gamut of analysis, group therapy, and self-help but still found themselves struggling with issues of meaning, purpose, and fundamental life-direction. They had learned that although secular psychology addresses a great deal about how we come to be the way we are and how we might live more efficiently, it can offer nothing in terms of why we exist or how we should use our lives. So increasing numbers of people began to turn back towards the world of the spirit.

Evangelical and Pentecostal movements proliferated dramatically. They offered more direct experiences of faith, and they gave clear prescriptions of how to live in awareness of Spirit. Charismatic renewal groups sprang up in the most surprising places, attracting a wide variety of people with their promise of direct, immediate, felt contact with the Holy Spirit. Simultaneously, many people turned to the religions of the Orient, which also promised more experience and deeper realization of a connectedness with the ultimate source of life. And most recently, people have started coming back for more traditional spiritual direction.

They have found the church ill-prepared. Protestants have almost no tested and accepted methods of individual spiritual direction, and Roman Catholics have discovered that many of their methods seem poorly equipped to respond to the complex needs of modern people. Thus within the past decade an energetic push has been undertaken to reclaim the old traditions of spiritual guidance and to integrate them with fresh ways of understanding modern spiritual searching. Spiritual direction training programs are springing up in centers across the country, and a new literature is emerging.

It is not an easy undertaking. The process of spiritual guidance continually raises deep theological questions. As but one example, it is clear that there is need for training in these disciplines. Yet one has to question how much of spiritual guidance can really be taught. Is it not in fact a charism, a gift of the Spirit? Denominational differences raise further questions, as does the modern cultural milieu, which has included so much psychology, secularization, moral fragmentation, and artificiality in managing human awareness. The issue of how psychology and spirituality interrelate in this contemporary situation is one of the more pressing challenges that must be faced by anyone who is called to offer spiritual guidance. There was a time when psychological phenomena were seen only in spiritual terms. Then we went through a period in which spirituality was often seen in psychological terms. Now, what?

Much is being written in this area. Many authors have reclaimed the rich resources of Jungian psychology in an attempt to integrate psyche and spirit into a comprehensible whole. Others have rediscovered the works of Roberto Assagioli, who proposed a psycho-spiritual model called psychosynthesis. Still others, like Thomas Hora and M. Scott Peck, have attempted to forge their own modern integrations. These many enterprises are both helpful and confusing, and will be so for some time to come. But the work is going on, and some of us are rediscovering an ancient truth in the process. We are learning that an enlightened appreciation of the eternal mystery behind our confusion may be of far greater value than any achievement we can make in trying to "figure things out."

At a conference on spiritual direction in the summer of 1980 Krister Stendahl spoke of the need for a new language to deal with modern spirituality and all of its ramifications.[2] A fresh language is certainly in order, for this is where much of our confusion is rooted. Who knows, for example, whether you and I mean the same thing when we say "Spirit"? Perhaps it is neither possible nor necessary that we agree completely, but we at least need to make our differences understandable. One of the more striking examples of this, for me, has occurred in my many interactions with Jungian psychologists. When we speak of Spirit it seems we are all in agreement until the question is put, "What is the source of Spirit?" Then we begin to confound each other about the relationship between Spirit, soul, and psyche. The differences, we find, go deeper than semantics. Jung's writings portrayed Spirit, soul, and even God as synonymous with, or secondary to, psyche and the unconscious.[3] To my understanding, psyche consists of a group of human mental functions, individual and collective, that are energized by spirit, and ultimately created and sustained by God. As such, it represents only one facet of soul. The new language, when it comes, needs to be able to sharpen these subtleties so our differences can be understood. Most importantly, I feel, it must be a language that permits and appreciates mystery without "solving" it.

As might be expected, a number of new "schools" of spiritual direction are being formed and refined in this modern struggle through the confusion. There are contemplative schools, holding up the numinous, mysterious reality of God that is touched in image-less silence. There are more psychological schools, emphasizing the discovery of the divine through dreams, images, and sensations. There are schools evolving that focus on healing, scripture, consciousness, social justice, and other specific attributes of the Spirit. There is still much confusion here, but there is also great enrichment. There will probably be heresy, but there will also be movement towards clarity.

Some Definitions

I do not propose the definitions that follow as absolute or theologically final. They are set forth only for the purpose of clarifying the orientation from which my subsequent discussion will come.

Soul, for me, reflects the essence of one's existence. In the sense of the Hebrew *nephesh* it represents the whole, living being of an individual person. Thus it is manifested through, rather than divorced from, body, mind, or any other facet of one's being. *Spirit* means to me the vital, dynamic force of being, that which is given by God and brings the soul into living reality. This understanding is for me compatible with the ancient terms *ruach, pneuma, spiritus,* and the Sanskrit *prāṇa.* Spirit implies energy and power. As our discussion proceeds, it will be important to differentiate the "good" Spirit that is more clearly a power of and towards God, from a variety of "evil" spirits, or other motive forces that tend to impel or propel us away from a rightful realization of our true relationship with God. Such differentiation is the essential function of *spiritual discernment.*[4]

Spiritual formation is a rather general term referring to all attempts, means, instructions, and disciplines intended towards deepening of faith and furtherance of spiritual growth. It includes educational endeavors as well as the more intimate and in-depth processes of spiritual direction.

Spiritual guidance can apply to any situation in which people receive help, assistance, attention, or facilitation in the process of their spiritual formation. This applies not only to deepening one's personal realization of relationship to God, but also to the dynamic living-out of that realization in the actions of daily life. Spiritual guidance can come through almost any conceivable channel. Certainly it can occur in church or other religious community settings, but it can also come from friends, family, coworkers, scripture, nature, art, and a multitude of other sources.

When spiritual guidance occurs in a formal, one-to-one relationship with another individual, it can be called *spiritual direction*. In the classic form of spiritual direction there is a director and a directee, the one helping the other to discern the work of the Lord in his or her life and to distinguish among the various forces or "spirits" which seem to beckon in different directions. In classic Roman Catholic or Eastern tradition, the director may be seen in either of two ways: as a "master" in a manner not unlike the Oriental guru, or more simply as an informed human being who represents a channel of grace. In either case it is generally assumed that the "real" director is the Holy Spirit, manifested through the relationship in a graced way. In times past, most—though by no means all—spiritual directors were clergy or religious. It appears that the modern rediscovery of the importance of spiritual direction is also including a reclaiming of the understanding that lay people are as readily and legitimately called and gifted for this discipline as are the ordained.

Spiritual direction is an old—some would say archaic—term that has seen considerable misuse and misunderstanding. Most Protestants and increasing numbers of modern Catholics have trouble with its authoritarian connotations. Although there have indeed been directors who maintained excessive dominance over their directees, a correct understanding considers a director not as one who gives orders but rather as one who points directions.

This pointing of direction becomes truly understandable only with an appreciation of the central role that discernment plays in spiritual direction. Anyone on an identified spiritual path experiences a variety of pullings and pushings, inclinations and disinclinations, attractions and repulsions that affect the direction he or she will follow. For example, as I have been working on this book I have felt a pull to spend less of my time in formal prayer and more on writing. Should I follow that inclination, or remain firmly disciplined in the time I set aside for prayer? Is this feeling a legitimate calling of God, a self-generated excuse to avoid prayer, or the sly work of some "other" force? This is a matter for discernment. It seems relatively minor compared with major vocational decisions or significant encounters with evil, but it demonstrates that discernment—as I understand it—has to do with finding and choosing the appropriate directions to follow in response to felt callings, leadings, and inclinations. In the spiritual life, we must make such discernments constantly, choosing our directions with care, consideration, and prayer. But because of our inherent personal blind spots and self-deceptions, and because of our vulnerability to deception from outside forces, it is necessary to have help. Thus the spiritual director aids us in finding our proper directions.

Still, a large number of people prefer the term "spiritual friend" as a way of avoiding the authoritarian connotations of "director." In general, I feel spiritual friendship can be seen as synonymous with spiritual direction, but one must be careful about the meaning. The notion of friendship can raise the issue of increasing mutuality in the relationship. This is a divergence from the classical model that can have both positive and negative consequences. It is not uncommon nowadays to encounter spiritual guidance relationships that are truly mutual, where two or even more people come together with no one being identified as "the authority." They provide guidance, discernment, and suggestions for each other at a completely "co-equal" level.

While such mutuality encourages greater intimacy and sharing among the parties, by removing the structure of the more formal relationship it courts the danger of turning spiritual direction into a "spiritual conversation" in which there is little accountability, direct confrontation, or precision in discernment. As in psychotherapy, mutuality can interfere with perspective. This is not to say that mutual spiritual relationships are destructive, but their lack of structure can sometimes foster unneeded distraction. One middle-ground alternative is mutual spiritual direction, a formal, structured relationship in which specific time is allotted during which one person acts as the director and the other the directee, after which the roles are reversed.

Another form that is becoming increasingly recognized and affirmed is group spiritual direction. Here one or two people guide a group on a formal, structured basis. The group members may support each other's journeys and offer insights and directions, but the leadership must remain recognized and definitive in order to warrant the label "direction." More loosely structured or shared-leadership groups may be considered forms of guidance or friendship but not direction. Group settings offer a broad range of support and perspective not available in individual direction, but they also lack some of the personal intimacy and in-depth discernment possibilities of individual direction.[5]

With the recent rise of popular interest in spirituality, some confusion has arisen concerning terminology for spiritual disciplines. Here again, the difficulty is often that popular minds have come up with understandings quite different from one another and from classic traditions. For example, *meditation* in the classic sense refers to a process of quiet reflection and thinking about some topic. This is contrasted with *contemplation,* a state of release from thought and image that has a very transcendent quality. In the popular mind, these understandings are sometimes totally reversed. One speaks of contemplating a thing, such as a navel, and meditation is often seen as including a wide variety of states of awareness ranging from visual imagery to open, spacious emptiness. I much prefer the classic understandings of these terms, as do most of the modern authorities in the field. The classic terminology is much more precise and allows for distinctions between humanly achieved and God-given states of awareness that the popular usage does not.

Things can become even more confusing when one begins to speak of *prayer.* Popularly, prayer is taken to mean a silent or spoken verbal interchange with God, and thus as somewhat different from meditation or contemplation. But in the classic sense, verbal prayer, meditation, contemplation, and even fasting and other ascetical disciplines are all considered different forms of prayer. A helpful distinction can be made here between verbal prayer and quiet prayer. Disciplines such as fasting are sometimes called body prayer.

Here again, the classic terminology seems preferable to me, but some modern distinctions can be helpful. For example, with the wide variety of meditational techniques now available, prayer seems more determined by intent than by content. A person may use a quiet, centering, relaxing technique as a way of deepening realization of being-in-God. This is prayer. But the very same technique might be used to ease psychological tension, to prepare for a difficult task, or to lower blood pressure or relieve a headache. These would not be prayer. In my understanding, prayer always needs to have some specific intent towards God.

There is also a modern confusion about the terms *contemplation* and *intuition*. In its classic sense, intuition is essentially synonymous with contemplation; it is a state free from thought, devoid of personal projections and imagery—a clear perception of things-as-they-truly-are. This is a far cry from the popular usage of intuition as a "hunch" or "sixth sense." Yet to further complicate matters, spiritual growth is often accompanied by the discovery of deep, subtle perceptions and insights that do not come into awareness through the usual sensory or ideational routes. While it is not etymologically sound, I do use the word "intuitive" to describe these subtle senses. Thus, for me, there is a difference between intuition and intuitive perception.

Finally, two different basic approaches to spirituality need to be clarified. In all traditions there is a way of viewing spirituality that emphasizes the importance of images, symbols, and sensations. This kind of spirituality, classically known as kataphatic, has always been the most popular. In it one seeks deeper realization of God through visions, feelings, imagery, words, and other sensate or symbolic forms of experience. The second way emphasizes the truth of God that lies behind, beyond, or hidden within all sensory or intellectual representations. This is known as the apophatic way. Evangelical and charismatic Christianity, popular Hinduism, and much of Tantric Buddhism represent markedly kataphatic spiritualities. At the other extreme, one might find the Christian mysticism of John of the Cross and Meister Eckhardt, the silence of Quaker Meeting, and the emptiness of Zen Buddhism, which are distinctly apophatic spiritualities.

In nearly all traditions one will find elements of both apophatic and kataphatic approaches, overlapping, but with one of the two in dominance. In most cases the kataphatic way will predominate, for as we shall see, there are elements of the apophatic approach that are deeply threatening from both psychological and spiritual standpoints. It should also be noted that most people who wind up with an apophatic orientation have passed through a number of kataphatic experiences or "phases" on their way. Younger people and individuals just beginning the process of intentional spiritual searching almost invariably start off with a kataphatic orientation. They seek substantial experience, sensate assurance of their relationship with the divine, and they expect this to occur through the usual and familiar media of senses, imagery, and thought. Sometimes people will continue to seek out such sensory experience for years before developing any deep appreciation of the mystery behind and beyond experience.

I am aware that I have made the apophatic approach sound more sophisticated or "mature" than the kataphatic in this discussion. This is my bias, but it should be acknowledged that the ultimate value of a person's approach to spiritual growth is finally the business of that person and God. Regardless of orientation, it is important that spiritual directors have a deep appreciation of the benefits and risks of both kinds of spirituality. Extremes of the kataphatic approach can produce endless fascination with imagery or thought, thus obscuring the divine source of all experience. Similarly, apophatic extremism can lead to life-denying and antiincarnational distortions.

From the standpoint of the direction relationship itself, it seems to me that a person with a solely kataphatic approach simply cannot provide apophatic guidance. Similarly, one with a severe apophatic bias may not be able to affirm the helpful images and experiences encountered in the spiritual growth of most directees. These observations have been accurate in my experience, but to put them into words like this is perhaps to place too much emphasis on the human characteristics of the spiritual director. If indeed the true director is the Holy Spirit working through grace, then perhaps the director's personal orientation is really of relatively minor importance. Still, it does seem clear to me that the director can interfere with the directee's growth through carelessness or through lack of discretion or humility. This can happen in a variety of ways. Perhaps the most common is the director's attempt to do too much, to take over or somehow commandeer the course of the directee's development. Another especially acute and modern problem occurs when the director cannot clearly differentiate between spiritual guidance and psychological counseling or therapy.

Spiritual Direction and Psychotherapy

There are many similarities between spiritual direction and psychotherapy, but they are fundamentally different undertakings. In the modern state of flux among spiritual and psychological interests, it is very important to keep the distinctions as clear as possible. It is very tempting to blur these differences in the name of integration, but to do so is to risk psychologizing the process of spiritual direction.[6] While the notion of combining psychological and spiritual care into a holistic approach to growth or healing is a noble ideal, in practice it takes great maturity and vigilance to avoid turning spiritual direction into a form of pastoral-psychological counseling that misses the spiritual mark. Psychological methods and attitudes are far more objective and tangible than their spiritual counterparts, and it is all too easy for both director and directee to be seduced into extensive psychological exploration at the expense of attention to the numinous and delicate calling-forth qualities of spirituality.

Yet it is obvious that all people entering spiritual direction have psychological concerns that have an intimate impact on their spirituality. To attempt too strict a separation, to try to divorce mind from spirit, would be artificial and not at all helpful. We are human souls, with body, mind, and spirit all reflecting facets of our unified being. To look to the spirit without also addressing the mind is as absurd as caring for the mind without attending to physical health. Thus, some kind of balanced attitude is necessary, one that can keep a perspective on all facets of a person and avoid both fascination and denial. For the purposes of this discussion, we will examine the differences between psychotherapy and spiritual direction in the light of content and intent. Further differences will emerge in subsequent chapters.[7]

Content

The most obvious difference in content between psychotherapy and spiritual direction is that the former focuses more on mental and emotional dimensions (thoughts, feelings, moods, and so on) while the latter focuses more precisely on spiritual issues such as prayer life, religious experiences, and sense of relationship to God. The primary danger in bringing these dimensions together is that mental and emotional concerns may kidnap the gentle spiritual attentiveness required of both director and directee. Some modern "psycho-spiritualities" rationalize this kind of seduction by saying that mind, emotions, relationships, and all other aspects of a person are ultimately spiritual and thereby worthy of primary attention in a direction relationship. While this is certainly true in a metaphysical sense, it gives license to call anything spiritual guidance. According to this view, anything that comes up in direction is a spiritual matter, and any and all responses to it are spiritual responses. Psychoanalysis, Gestalt Therapy, primal screaming, sex therapy, biofeedback treatment, tranquilizing and antidepressant drug therapies, assertiveness training, and even psychosurgery could be included as forms of spiritual guidance if this line of thought were taken to its extreme. At some point of course, it would have to be recognized that any real attention to spirituality had been lost in such undertakings, but this realization might well not occur until after the divergence had become severe.

One example of this divergence that actually does happen with some frequency has to do with the use of dream work in spiritual direction. It is the nature of dreams to be endlessly complex. The more one analyzes them the more dreams one remembers and the more symbolic they seem to become. Before long it is possible to be devoting nearly all one's efforts and attention to the dream exploration. At this point, the balanced recognition that dreams are only one of many valuable sources of spiritual and psychological insight has been lost, and the dreams themselves have become a source of extensive distraction. The means have eclipsed the end. Similar distortions can easily occur in spiritual guidance that focuses excessively on extrasensory psychic experiences, special spiritual powers, deliverance, or any other phenomena that seem especially exciting, dramatic, or meaningful.

It is a good rule of thumb for spiritual directors to ask themselves, What truly constitutes our spiritual concern here? Am I really being attentive to the Lord in this? What things are getting in the way of our simple, humble intention towards the working of the Holy Spirit in this person's life? All human experience can be said to be spiritual in the largest sense, but spiritual direction should deal primarily with those qualities that seem most clearly and specifically spiritual, those that reveal the presence or leadings of God, or evidence of grace, working most directly in a person's life. This becomes increasingly important as spiritual direction progresses over time with any given individual. In the course of spiritual maturation, concern with superficial psychological experience must give way to a much more basic concern for the discernment of good and evil.

Thus, it is to be expected that spiritual direction will give primary attention to such things as the directee's inclinations in relation to personal prayer life and other ascetical practices like fasting and simplification in life; to senses of God's presence, absence, or callings; to experiences of fundamental meaning; to personal longings for God; and to the multiplicity of factors that seem most to help or hinder freedom for fullness of living in God's reality. Many other topics and issues will naturally surface in the course of any spiritual direction session, but ideally they should be examined for their relevance to the above kinds of concerns. In other words, all of life's experiences can appear legitimately in spiritual direction, but they need to be seen in the light of spiritual concern, and at all costs they should not be allowed to eclipse that light.

Intent

Most traditional psychotherapy does not see itself as facilitating the growth of persons in their realization and expression of divine truth. In general, psychotherapy hopes to encourage more efficient living, and its values and intentions often reflect those that prevail in the culture at any given time. For example, psychotherapy often seeks to bolster an individual's capacity to gratify needs and desires and to achieve a sense of autonomous mastery over self and circumstance. Both of these orientations are quite prominent in modern society as a whole. In contrast, spiritual direction—at least in its more mature forms—seeks liberation from attachments and a self-giving surrender to the discerned power and will of God. This means that at some point spiritual direction will turn in opposition to many of the cultural standards and values that psychotherapy supports.

A deeper divergence of intent can be seen in the different attitudes psychotherapy and spiritual guidance hold towards the manner in which growth, healing, and liberation actually take place. In the harshest medical model of psychiatry, the physician assumes the role of healer while the patient remains at best a compliant object whose deficiencies are corrected. In more humanistic psychotherapies, therapist and client form a healing team together. They see their mutual interactions as being responsible for any growth or healing that may take place. In spiritual direction however, the true healer, nurturer, sustainer, and liberator is the Lord, and the director and directee are seen as hopeful channels, beneficiaries, or expressions of grace for each other. This is a radical difference, and one that cannot be overemphasized.

There are, to be sure, psychotherapists and counselors who see themselves humbly, hoping to be instruments of divine will rather than of personal ego, or who at least try to keep their personal will in accordance with their discernments of God's will. To date however, it must be acknowledged that in the actual practice of therapy, such orientations represent more the exception than the rule. The important consideration here is that while effective psychotherapy can occur with the intent of human achievement, any spiritual direction that loses its sense of human subservience is bound to be distorted. Such distortion occurs far more frequently than most of us would care to admit. The seeds of its potential are in every such thought as *I have to help this person*, or *I must do something to make this person see things differently*, or even in *Together you and I will overcome this obstacle*. In each of these thoughts the power of God, even that which works *through* us, is ignored.

The potential for evil here is immense, and it poses one of the greatest challenges to vigilance for the spiritual director. When we examine the most destructive aberrations that have occurred in the name of religion throughout history, we see the recurrent phenomenon of spiritual leaders taking destiny upon themselves, playing God, substituting personal mastery for surrender to divine will.

Of course at the other extreme lies the risk of self-restraining quietism, a less violent but still destructive alternative in which one avoids one's own graced potential for action by refraining from doing anything at all. If examined closely, both of these extremes can be seen as resulting from excessive willfulness, the former by exaggerating and aggrandizing personal power, and the latter by forcibly denying and restricting it. The one denies the transcendence of God; the other denies God's immanence and human responsiveness *to* God.

As I struggle to appreciate these extremes and the balanced potential that lies between them, I find it helpful to think of the ways we use our hands. There is a natural, flowing way in which we use our hands when we are simply doing something that needs to be done. Even in definitive and dramatic action our hands can be this way, reflecting their inherent cooperation with, and integral connectedness to, the fullness of our bodies. This way comes naturally to us, and it can be capable of great strength as well as serene quietude. But at other times, when we become overly self-conscious and preoccupied, our hands turn into jerky, contrived things that grasp and claw, clench and shove, meddle and manipulate. This is very like the way we ourselves become when we bind ourselves to personal desire-attachments or strive for autonomous control and mastery. At still other times we sit on our hands, forcibly and brutally preventing their movement. Then we are witholding ourselves from living interaction with the world around us. Whether we do this out of fear or rebellion or through some misguided facsimile of surrender, we do it to ourselves. At some level this self-enforced passivity is just as willful as our attempts to play God and master destiny. It's just that the drive towards mastery is much more seductive in our present autonomy-intoxicated culture.

In my opinion, the relationship between personal and divine will is the most fierce and treacherous confrontation faced by modern spiritual guides and leaders. It demands that they be constantly attentive to and critical of their own spiritual inclinations, and it absolutely requires that they have competent spiritual direction for themselves. The question is deceptively simple to ask and exquisitely difficult to answer: Am I truly seeking to do Thy will . . . or mine?

2. Incarnation: Developmental and Biological Considerations

Humans are physical beings. We are *incarnated*. The life of our bodies and minds is both an expression of and a prerequisite for our growth as souls. In the process of this growth, it appears that there are certain common phases through which our minds and bodies pass. There are clear stages of infancy, childhood, adolescence, adulthood, and maturity, each resting upon the one preceding and each associated with certain characteristics of physical ability, mental and emotional capacity, and to some extent, spiritual awareness. Such stages are real, and understanding them can give us some perspective on the deeper nature of ourselves and each other.

Here again though, we must take care not to overdo. The stages of human growth are by no means absolute, and there are no hard-and-fast criteria by which their ultimate health or goodness can be measured. For example, while it is true that some distortion of early experience can be identified in many cases of mental disorder, there are also innumerable examples of childhood trauma and deprivation that seem to strengthen, rather than harm, a person's later adjustment.

This uncertainty is even more pertinent in the realm of human spiritual development. Several authors have posed that spiritual growth follows a series of stages similar to those of personality development.[1] In many cases it does indeed seem that such a progression takes place, from childhood's narcissistic relationships with God-images through adolescent rebellion and adult efficiency to a more compassionate and accepting experience of faith in maturity. But there are always exceptions. Sometimes children manifest perceptions of God that are far more mature than those of their most sophisticated elders. Similarly, narcissistic distortions of faith can occur at any age and may, in fact, be especially common among "mature" adults who have identified themselves as intentional spiritual seekers.

Thus it is wise to hold all concepts of stages in spiritual growth very loosely, using them only at the most gross levels of understanding and remembering constantly that the manifestations of grace in a person's life can never stop surprising us. Among those spiritual directors who have some understanding of popular psychology, there is a common assumption that one must have arrived at a certain level of emotional maturity before effective use can be made of spiritual guidance or intentional spiritual disciplines. A popular way of stating this is "One must have an ego before it can be given up." While this makes a great deal of logical and psychological sense, there are so many exceptions to it that—to me at least—its usefulness as a dictum is very questionable. There are a great many souls walking among us who could be psychiatrically labeled as neurotic or psychotic yet who manifest such deepness and clarity of faith that they could well be *our* spiritual guides.

In practice then, I feel it would be unfair and ignorant to refuse to see someone in spiritual direction simply because that person has some mental disorder, immaturity of emotions, or instability of personality. The discernment of readiness for direction cannot be made on this kind of basis. Only in talking intimately with people and prayerfully reflecting on the divine process in their lives can one decide about the advisability of various forms of spiritual guidance. In other words, we must attend to the soul and not be railroaded by concern about some partial aspect of a person.

In some instances emotional immaturity or psychiatric disorder can create such self-preoccupation or perceptual distortion that an individual simply cannot address the nuances of his or her spiritual life. To burden such persons with specific spiritual disciplines or questions might only serve to compound their confusion. At other times people may come for spiritual direction when their real need (and perhaps what they are being called to) is therapy or counseling. Further, there are many situations in which a person can be in psychotherapy and spiritual direction simultaneously.

In the vast majority of cases, psychological difficulties need not interfere at all with spiritual direction. Instead, they often serve as gifts for enrichment of one's spiritual sensitivities. This is especially true, for example, in addictions (as discussed in Chapter 7) or in situations of anxiety or depression that contain deep existential concerns.[2] Many times I have seen people forced by anxiety to confront issues of meaning, consciousness, self, and God in ways that have led to deep spiritual openings, levels they would never have faced had they not been deeply distressed with their lives.

An understanding of levels or stages of maturation can be extremely helpful from the conceptual standpoint of thinking about spiritual growth, but in practice each person must be seen afresh on each occasion. We may have our psychological stages, but God does not always seem to work through them in accordance with our predictions. Again, I feel the best practical guideline here is that we always be willing to be surprised by grace.

Four Forces in Human Spirituality

From another viewpoint, four primary forces can be seen to impinge upon spiritual growth. From the human side of things, the first of these is our spiritual longing. An awareness of need for deeper realization of God can surface at many points in the course of life. Often it is some event, circumstance, or life-passage that seems to prompt us towards introspection and reflection about the meaning of our lives. This may happen in the course of a crisis, or when most of the crises have passed and in the luxury of security we begin to ask What's it all for? Or it can just happen, spontaneously and without any apparent human cause.

Spiritual longing often takes the form of a desire to re-unite with the ultimate Source of being, as if we know vaguely that at some primeval level we are in and of God, and God is in and through us. Usually this craving for re-union is associated with a desire to realize and express divine, unconditional love. Sometimes these longings for God seem to be triggered by a visionary or unitive experience, but again they often just seem to happen.

A second force, clearly overlapping with and presumably causing our longing for God, is God's longing for us. This can be discerned most clearly when our own spiritual hunger arises for no apparent reason. Often it can be seen in retrospect, behind many of the crises or other life-experiences that seem to prompt us into spiritual searching. It is also evident in the innocent faith of children and "simple" people.

The third is a force that opposes our growth towards deeper realization and freedom in spiritual life. It is our own internal fears of and resistances to spiritual realization. Spiritual growth demands much that we are unwilling to give. It threatens to loosen our cherished attachments, to change or even dissolve our frozen images of ourselves, and to reveal certain truths about ourselves that we are loath to admit. Further, it asks sacrifices of our time, energy, and resources; it demands our very hearts. It should not be surprising to find ourselves resisting that which we consciously most desire, or distorting spiritual truth into self-contrived figments that we hope might give us fulfillment without sacrifice. As we shall see in Chapter 5, many of these resistances occur in the form of classic psychological defense mechanisms like repression, denial, and displacement. The spiritual director is considerably enabled by familiarity with these defensive maneuvers.

The fourth force, which also functions in opposition to spiritual growth, comes not so much from the personal psyche as from sources that can only be called evil. Evil takes many forms. It can be expressed through cultural and societal attitudes that encourage attachment to desire and self-aggrandizement. It can occur as the theological *demonic*, in which something other than God becomes our ultimate concern. And, especially in the course of intentional spiritual searching, evil can surface in the form of real spiritual forces (spirits) that seek to divert and sabotage our journey towards deeper realization of God's truth and will. In spiritual guidance, it often seems that this fourth force becomes increasingly important as one matures, and with it comes an increasing need for careful discernment.

Whatever its specific manifestations may be, it seems to me that evil always functions to subvert one's surrender to God, seeking to turn it into a capitulation to darkness and willfulness. Theologically one might see that evil forces are ultimately of or at least permitted by God, but from the standpoint of human experience they clearly work to turn one's attention and intention away from God.

At any given point in life, these four forces can be seen as impinging upon each other in a dynamic interplay. This interplay determines both the content and the nature of one's spiritual sensitivity, and the balance may change and shift in a variety of ways over time. It could be said that the spiritual director attempts, in his or her humanity, to take the pulse of this balance and, through graced discernment, assist in its inclination towards God. As we shall discuss later, this discernment process is different from "diagnosis" and the healing, guiding, reconciling, and correcting influence of the director is different from "treatment." In times past, spiritual direction was associated with the "cure of souls." In spite of its beauty, I feel this is one term that has become so contaminated by modern medical and scientific attitudes that its popular usage can be seriously misleading. Perhaps the idea of the cure of souls can be held quietly in one's heart, but only if one is deeply secure in the knowledge of what cure really is, where it really comes from, and what is really being cured.

Biological Considerations

Presumably the brain is the incarnated mediator of human spiritual experience. It consists of billions of nerve cells interconnected in literally countless ways. Its outer layer of cells, the cortex, is the repository of thought, sense perception, memory, and intentional body movement. Deep inside the brain lie other systems of cells that mediate emotions, physical desires, body temperature, metabolic rate, and level of wakefulness. All of these areas are interconnected and mutually influence each other through incredibly complex combinations of facilitation, inhibition, and feedback.[3]

The brain functions electrochemically. Signals travel along nerve cell fibers electrically, and pass from one nerve cell to another by means of specific chemicals that are secreted and absorbed at the connection points between cells. In a sense then, all thinking, feeling, and aspiring; all memory, hope, and sensation; every bit of human experience from the simplest reflex to the most lofty aspiration is dependent upon the electrochemical functioning of nerve cells. However, this is not to say that all experience is *created* by these cells.

Specific changes in brain chemicals have been shown to be associated with depression and mania, with organization and disorganization of thought processes, and with feelings of pleasure and discomfort. But it is impossible to distinguish whether the subjective thought or feeling is the effect or the cause of electrochemical activity within the cells. Indeed, it is possible to cause a memory or feeling to enter awareness by stimulating a specific area of the brain with electrodes, just as it is possible to choose intentionally to think about a certain topic by the exertion of one's subjective will. But there is still no way of ascertaining the real difference between biophysical changes and subjective experiences. Do chemicals create thoughts? Do thoughts create chemicals? Do they somehow create each other? Does God create both? I suspect that the answer is yes to all four questions. The brain mediates experience in ways so intimately bound to experience itself that the two cannot be separated.

Biological Manipulation

Historically there has been a rather comical effort to find a part of the brain that could be identified as "the seat of the soul." Of course this anatomical figment has not been discovered. This is fortunate, for if the soul were found to be such a tangible and objective entity, we would almost certainly attempt to alter it in some way. Many modern scientists now seem to be coming round to the more ancient spiritual appreciation of soul as the essence of individual being, the mysterious reality of how our brains and bodies exist and behave. Yet paradoxically, as we discover more about the brain, we are increasingly tempted to try to reduce our spiritual realities to matters of chemistry.

Perhaps the most obvious example of this was the great psychedelic craze of the 1960s. Discovering that certain chemicals could alter awareness through their effects upon the brain, many people entertained the notion that drugs might be a vehicle for greater realization of God. The psychedelic drugs affect brain chemistry directly, thereby sometimes producing states of perception and experience that are very similar to naturally occurring spiritual experiences. Similar alterations can happen with extremes of ascetical practice, such as fasting and other bodily or sensory deprivations, and in association with schizophrenia, mania, and other psychiatric conditions. Such observations supported the already existing tendency to believe that with sufficient mastery of our brains we humans might be able to engineer our own spiritual salvation. We could break the habitual and bodily chains that keep us from full realization of ultimate reality.

But this is proving to be a passing fancy. While it is certainly possible to alter our thinking, feeling, perception, and qualities of awareness in a multitude of artificial ways, thus creating a host of strange and wondrous experiences, none of this has seemed to produce any true spiritual nourishment. At best such enterprises serve to dislodge frozen preconceptions of the world and to whet the appetite for "the real thing." At worst, they stuff awareness full of contents utterly lacking in sustenance that obscure the realities of daily life.[4]

This conclusion holds, I propose, for all contrived experiences—from drugs to sensory deprivation, from brain-wave biofeedback to guided imagery, from extreme asceticism even to forms of prayer or meditation designed to achieve certain psychological states. This is not to say that all such activities are to be scorned. There may be a time and a place for humanly originated "appetizers," and certainly there is value in learning how to relax in prayer or how to open one's sensitivities to subtler levels of image and insight. But this is not the same thing as trying to achieve spiritual growth. Intentional practices such as prayer, meditation, fasting, mindfulness, and charity are very important in personal spiritual development, but they need to be seen as ways of encouraging oneself to be more freely and deeply and directly responsive to God, rather than ways of engineering one's own salvation.

This is sometimes a very difficult distinction to make. Once we find the capacity to alter our state of awareness, it is almost impossible to avoid being caught up in the hope of being able to commandeer ourselves towards God—or towards some other destination of our own choosing. Yet, in such attempts, all that happens is egocentric frustration. The fact that we are learning more effective ways of influencing our brains, bodies, and biochemistries means that we can be more willing, healthful, and responsive recipients of God's call to us. It does not mean we are better able to play God.

Psychophysiology and Spiritual Growth

In recent years there have been many attempts to establish correlations between human spiritual experience and such psychophysiological factors as brain-wave patterns, right/left brain balance, life stages, and personality styles. All these endeavors have proved fascinating, for at the most primitive levels of study there do seem to be connections.

Many spiritual experiences that have transcendent or unitive qualities seem to be associated with brain-wave patterns that are relatively slow and synchronous. Spiritual growth, at some stages, seems to be characterized by enhancement of the intuitive/aesthetic sensitivities, which have been associated with the right side of the brain. Certain life stages, notably those associated with identity formation and "midlife crisis" seem especially ripe for spiritual conversion experiences. And intuitive/feeling personality styles seem to have an easier time dealing with certain spiritual subtleties than do personalities of a more intellectual or obsessive orientation.

Such hints of connections can stimulate an almost irresistible passion to master spiritual destiny. If we could only learn how to produce the proper brain waves . . . if we could discover a way of balancing the brain's right and left hemispheres. . . . Or perhaps we could set up spiritual guidance programs for people in midlife crisis . . . and develop special disciplines for teaching thought-oriented people how to be more aesthetically sensitive. Any of these endeavors might be of value in its own right, but to see them as ways of accomplishing spiritual growth runs close to the danger of trying to play God. In addition, such thinking is often frankly in error.

For example, more precise observations show that the slow, harmonious brain waves associated with certain spiritual experiences are also associated with hypnotic trances and a wide range of other subjective experiences. And it has been shown that the left brain can take over the functions of the right; that spiritual conversions are not really determined by life stage; and that many intellect-oriented people experience profound spiritual openings, while many of their more intuitive peers do not.

Thus, while the research goes on and we become enriched by it, the relationship between director and directee must also go on as a cherished, graced, and constantly surprising process in which we are participants but never masters. A person may be stuck in intellectualizing about faith, for example, and seem unable to experience anything. Although in trying to help that person we might be aided by our knowledge of personality types or brain workings, it is imperative that our knowledge or trying-to-help never obscure our attention to how God is already working in that person's life. Another individual may be very depressed or anxious, and although we may try to respond in an informed and caring way, we must not forget that what we are really about is the facilitation of that person's growth in God. Someone else may be in a crisis of life and relationship. Listening, hearing, perhaps even suffering with that person, we still must ask, Where is grace in this for you?

In essence then, legitimate spiritual guidance involves a full acceptance of the physical and psychological nature of human beings and an informed, caring response to the manifestations of that nature. But it is also continually and consciously rooted in mystery and in an awareness of graced furtherance of the person's life in and towards God.

3. Vision: Forms of Spiritual Experience

In traditional religious understanding, consciousness is intimately related to spirit and soul. According to these understandings, consciousness is not seen as limited to individual brain function, but as having much deeper and broader implications. Teresa of Avila's *Interior Castle,* a classic treatise on the spiritual dimensions of consciousness, describes how at its deepest levels consciousness reflects a profound in-touchness with the divine.

In this sense, consciousness represents a fundamental, and perhaps even universal, manifestation of the divine. I have found it useful to see human awareness as that portion of consciousness that is accessible to us and with which we identify ourselves and our individual existences. In other words, we "have" awareness; it is the atmosphere in which all experience occurs to us. But each of our individual awarenesses is rooted in a larger, common principle of consciousness, the full nature of which we can barely begin to appreciate. This larger consciousness "has" us. Although I do not equate this larger consciousness with God, it does sometimes seem to me an aspect of God.

Contents and Qualities of Awareness

By describing human awareness as an "atmosphere," I am raising another contrast between spiritual and psychological attitudes. Psychology has traditionally been preoccupied with the "contents" of this atmosphere, the thoughts, feelings, sense perceptions, and imagery that occur within the matrix of awareness, and with the behavioral responses that take place in relationship to these contents. While spirituality is also concerned with these contents and behaviors, especially as they relate to spiritual growth, it also addresses the nature, quality, and source of human awareness and of all consciousness. In spiritual direction situations, one is not only interested in the specific thoughts, images, and perceptions a person might have about God, but also with the atmosphere in which such phenomena occur. This concern is helpful in considering whether a given experience is *of* God as well as *about* God. These deeper and more numinous dimensions of spiritual experience can hardly be touched by traditional psychological evaluation.

The "contents" (thoughts, images, desires, and the like) that may occur in prayer are as amenable to psychological examination as they are to spiritual discernment, and it is usually good to look at them from both perspectives. But there are other levels that are of special note in spiritual discernment, subtle hints and inclinations, formless qualities of the awareness in which the events occur, senses of the deep silent "background" out of which all interior experience takes form, and perceptions of the presence or absence of good or evil behind and around the manifest contents of awareness. Apophatic forms of spiritual direction focus more precisely on these subtle background qualities, but even strongly kataphatic approaches must take them into account in the process of legitimate discernment.

The spiritual evaluation of a specific experience, for example, might include a consideration of whether that experience was associated with an atmosphere of love and light or of emptiness and darkness. At these levels, standard psychiatric ways of analysis have very little use. A specific content of awareness may be subjected legitimately to psychological scrutiny regarding its symbolic significance and psychodynamic precursors, but the quality of awareness in which it occurred must be dealt with from a more specifically spiritual perspective.

This kind of sensitivity is not fully "teachable." It grows in large part out of one's personal interior experience in silence and prayer, and is refined through discernments in one's own spiritual direction. Further, it is manifested as part of the charism of spiritual guidance. This again underscores the necessity of being in direction oneself before offering it to others.

Experiences of Union

Two basic kinds of "content" experiences can be described. The first of these is the classic *unitive* experience in which all the activities that serve to define oneself are suspended, yet awareness remains open, clear, and vibrant. For the duration of such experiences there is no self-consciousness, no self/other distinction, no trying-to-do or-not-to-do, no aspiration, labeling, judgment, or differentiation. Thoughts may occur, but there is no self-defining act of thinking. Sense perceptions may appear with exceeding clarity, but there is no self-responding, no naming or evaluating of them.

Unitive experiences are widely misunderstood. For one thing, they are not forms of trance or dissociation in which one's self-image feels separated from normal sensory input. Self-image is preserved and awareness restricted in trances and dissociations. Nor are unitive experiences the same as "fusion" sensations in erotic love, in which awareness is condensed into such centered intensity that all other perceptions are excluded.[1] In true unitive experience the senses are wide open; the world presents itself with utter clarity, but there is no sense of separation of oneself from it. Certain drugs and other artificial conditions can stimulate "oceanic" sensations that may be confused with unitive experience. Here one's self-definition remains, and one is simply overawed by the immensity of some vast, panoramic perception. Finally, the self-image-losing qualities of true unitive experience differ from the ego-fragmentation seen in certain prepsychotic conditions. In the unitive state there is no sense of fragmentation or schism. While there may be a blurring of ego-boundaries in personality disintegration, one can always find a very definite sense of self—besieged and embattled though it may be—clinging to survival somewhere in awareness.

Unitive experiences often occur spontaneously, and often outside of obviously religious contexts. Many times they are quickly repressed or denied. Still, they constitute the basic form of spiritual experience, one in which a person, however briefly, actually experiences the reality of being rooted in oneness with all creation.

Unitive experiences are associated with a multitude of paradoxes. It is impossible, for example, for a person to recognize the experience at the time it is happening. To do so would imply a self-definition such as "I am experiencing union" or "This is happening to me." Such observations would, of course, immediately re-establish self-definition and preclude full unitive realization. Thus, unitive experiences can only really be identified in retrospect. Another paradox is involved in the fact that unitive experiences can never be personally achieved, because all thoughts or intents towards making the experience happen are inherently self-defining. It is possible to increase one's openness, receptivity, and responsiveness to unitive experiences, but it is not possible to make them happen.

An experience of union, of course, does not imply that an individual is really any more at one than before or after the experience. Rather, it must be understood that the experience constitutes a realization (in the literal sense) of an aspect of life that is constantly true but that goes unrecognized most of the time. In this regard, unitive experiences can be seen as one kind of *contemplative* state. In classic language they are a form of "infused" contemplation, that which comes solely as a gift, as compared to "acquired" contemplation, that which comes partly from personal effort and intention. Still, there are other forms of infused contemplation in which some self-image remains or in which awareness is more focused. It is not necessary to classify all these states here, but it is of value to recognize the two essential and fundamental qualities of full unitive experience, that *all* self-definition is suspended and that awareness is clear and *wide open,* excluding nothing. In practice one can examine the self-losing aspect of unitive experience by asking What was your sense of yourself during the experience? In the true experience, there will be *no* sense of self; self will be forgotten. Feelings like "I was dissolving" or "I belonged to everything" or "I expanded to include everything" or "I went out of myself to somewhere else" all indicate the continuation of self-definition and therefore the absence of true unitive experience. The degree of openness of awareness can be checked by asking Did you hear the birds (or other background sounds)? In full unitive experience there is no shutting-out of perception and no focusing of attention on this or that to the exclusion of something else.

Experiences in Which Self-Image Is Preserved

The second major category of spiritual experience is those characterized by the retention of self-definition. All spiritual experiences
that are not fully unitive fall into this group. One example is sensory experience in which one vividly sees, hears, or otherwise perceives something that has clear spiritual implications. Sensory experiences may range from intentional imagination or visualization
(called imagery) to spontaneous visions that seem to arise from
outside oneself. Meditation in which one imagines being involved
in a scripture story is an example of imagery. Paul's experience on
the road to Damascus is an example of a vision. Between these two
extremes lies a host of sensory possibilities. Some may begin as
intentional forms of meditation and take unexpected spontaneous
turns. Others may consist of hearing an inner voice uttering some
reassurance or challenge, or a subtle interior sense ("intuitive" in
the popular usage) of direction. Still others may involve seeing
light, feeling temperature changes, or perceiving some physical
sensation such as tremorous shaking or profound relaxation. A
somewhat related phenomenon is that of intellectual experience.
Often we tend to think of intellect and experience as two different
things, but in fact it is possible to have a direct and immediate
experience of one's own intellect. This is especially obvious when a
sudden insight or illumination is gained, or when something previously confusing is suddenly understood. More subtle forms of intellectual experience occur when one watches the mysterious ways
in which thoughts occur in awareness, how they interrelate, and
the manner in which they seem to disappear. Such experiences are
especially common in contemplative practice, which involves extensive meditation or quiet prayer.

Extrasensory experiences are also frequently encountered in the
course of spiritual practice. These may include any of the classic
parapsychological phenomena such as telepathy, precognition, out-
of-body experiences, the seeing of auras, and (rarely) telekinetic
experiences in which matter seems directly affected by spiritual or
psychic force.

Of a somewhat related nature are the classic Christian charismatic experiences, which include such phenomena as healing,

speaking in tongues, and prophecy. In addition, one may encounter the dramatic dissociative or trancelike states called "being slain by the Spirit." It is obvious that the interpretation of all these kinds of experiences, and to some extent their very nature, is very much determined by the context in which they occur. For example, experiences that would be called telepathic or precognitive in a secular setting might be seen as prophetic in many religious contexts. In addition, the differences often seem to go deeper than semantics. The actual quality of experience of spiritual healing, for example, may be quite different in a charismatic Christian context as compared with another cultural or religious setting. The former often includes a felt spiritual presence or force associated with love. In some other setting such a force may not be felt at all, or it may be experienced as having other properties, such as electrical or magnetic qualities. While there are many objective similarities among all such experiences, it is obvious that evaluation of such phenomena cannot legitimately occur without consideration of the person to whom and the context within which the experience happened.

Of course not all spiritual experiences are pleasant or reassuring. There are many that have a quality of darkness or fear. Here it is especially important to be able to distinguish between the "fear and trembling" that occurs as a natural human response to the awesome power of God, and the fear experienced in encounters with evil. These distinctions are not always easy, and are probably never absolute. There are qualities of encounter with God that are dark, empty, and "abysmal." A matter for exceedingly careful discernment, such experiences are usually associated with an underlying sense of goodness, love, or faith that remains constant or is even deepened by the experience. In contrast, encounters with decidedly evil forces are usually associated with a sense of very deep antagonism against one's faith or against one's inclination towards God. Further, discriminations cannot be fully made without consideration of the life-impact or "fruits" of various experiences, and often this means that one must wait and see what happens before making any kind of final statement. Arbitrary standards applied to such experiences are not generally effective, and the test involves a graced combination of wisdom, knowledge, patience, and prayerful attentiveness on the part of both director and directee.

Classically, the most dramatic encounters with evil take the form of *obsession,* an increasing internal preoccupation or fascination with the forces of darkness, or *possession,* in which one is actually taken over by some external evil force. Obsession may take the form of personal interest and investment in sorcery, witchcraft, magic, or other occult practices that are designed to invoke spiritual powers, or it may occur as an intense drive to combat such forces (the "spiritual warrior" theme taken to its negative extreme). The relationship between these two forms of fascination can easily be understood in the classic psychiatric concepts of projection and re-action formation. In projection, one invests something or someone else with one's own unwanted traits and then proceeds to fight them. In reaction formation, one does the exact opposite of one's basic desires. Thus, it is probably appropriate to be suspicious of any overzealous attempts to do combat with evil. Often this is a form of "protesting too much" that belies underlying inclinations in the opposite direction.

Possession occurs very rarely, and when it does it has often been preceded by an extensive and intense period of obsession. Posses-sion is associated with specific signs that have been spelled out in classic Roman Catholic and Anglican literature. Any responsible discernment of possession must finally involve evaluation by both spiritual and psychiatric experts, the former to test the phenom-enon by classic means and the latter to rule out psychological manifestations that may masquerade as external forces of evil. It is far more wise that the contemporary spiritual director know to whom to turn for consultation in such matters than to try to learn the fine points of diagnosis, exorcism, and the like.[2]

Experiences and Discernments

Of considerable concern in spiritual direction is the discernment of the nature and implications of these various spiritual experiences, and of the proper reactions or responses one should have to them. Classically, discernment involves distinguishing among inclinations that may be of God, of the evil spirit, or of oneself. A great deal has been written about the way psychological dynamics appear in the guise of religious experience, so much in fact that I feel it may have gone a bit too far. While it is true that many "spiritual" experiences are primarily generated from the psyche (and perhaps almost all of them are in some way mediated by it), I doubt that it helps to become overly preoccupied with arbitrary distinctions between what is "of the self" and what is "of God." The real question, I think, is whether the "self" aspects of an experience facilitate or hinder one's growth toward God, or whether they are consonant with or antagonistic towards God's will. To assume that something of the self must inherently be against God is to deny that aspect of ourselves that is made in God's image and to devalue our own intentionality towards God.

While there are many aspects of self that do impede and resist spiritual growth, there are many that would foster and enhance it. Too much emphasis on self-vs.-God encourages an artificial and erroneous dualism, rashly separating one's inner psychological experience from the workings of the Holy Spirit in our lives. The fact is, of course, that God often speaks to us and works in us through our psychological experience. Mediated and altered as they may be by our personal attachments and preconceptions, the manifestations of grace are as truly present in our subjective psychology as in a sunset or a rainbow. Further, preoccupation with considerations of psyche-vs.-God can lead, paradoxically, to an unintended preoccupation with the psyche itself. The human mind presents so much material to deal with that it can easily become a quagmire for the curious. Thus to invest oneself in separating psychodynamics from the revelations of God can become a distortion not unlike excessive spiritual warfare; it can become as much of a distraction as seeking God solely *through* psychology. Both extremes occur all too frequently in modern spiritual guidance because of our society's ambivalent obsession with psychology.

Here again, some balance of perspective is needed. Excessive preoccupation with psyche and evil—either from supportive or antagonistic standpoints—fosters a degree of self-consciousness and self-importance that is very likely to eclipse the ever-present mystery of God's truth. Discernments are essential, but it is not at all necessary or helpful to become attached to making them. If possible, it is best to see psychological phenomena such as dreams, fantasies, images, and thoughts as manifestations of God's potential in the same way that nature, art, relationships, and all other phenomena are. Gazing into an empty, blue sky, kneeling in prayer in a cathedral, and recalling memories associated with a dream can all be worthwhile spiritual explorations. They can also all be distractions from spiritual exploration. The beauty of the sky or the cathedral can create an absorption with sensate experience, just as dream analysis can create ego-absorption. (I must add here that if I were to choose among these, I would definitely prefer the blue sky.)

The importance of experiences lies not so much in their precise nature as in one's response to them. In part this represents a harkening back to an old principle of discernment that we have mentioned before, that of evaluating an experience in relation to its fruits. More deeply, however, we are speaking of remaining attentive to the mystery and reality of God *behind* all phenomena, refusing to allow superficial appearances to distract us from this central concern. We do a disservice to ourselves and others when we allow our interest in the nature of a phenomenon to obscure the mysterious wonder of the very existence of that phenomenon.

It was the recommendation of John of the Cross (in a manner similar to that of Gamaliel[3]) that one should not pay particular attention to any phenomena or experiences. If an experience were truly and directly of God, he felt, its truth would become evident naturally in one's life. If it were of something "else," it would certainly not be worthy of attention. Therefore, no special attention was necessary.

In practice, and perhaps especially in the practice of spiritual direction, such a constant and pure nonattention may not be possible. Certainly, experiences that involve a sense of calling or leading must be attended to with careful discernment. Further, the director must at least respond to a directee's interest in specific experiences. Especially in the early phases of spiritual growth, sensory experiences are very important as sources of motivation, energy, and aspiration. To deny their value would in most cases constitute a rejection of the directee's humanity, and in some instances it would amount to an attack on the directee's faith. Thus, while it is advisable not to "hop on board" with excessive curiosity or fascination about anything that presents itself in spiritual direction, a gentle attentiveness—attention without attachment—is called for.

Gentle and prayerful attention combined with good common sense and classic discernment methods are sufficient for most discriminations that need to be made regarding spiritual experiences.[4] If, for example, a specific experience is associated with a sense of increased willfulness, greater self-concern, or excessive fascination, its value quite obviously will need to be questioned. Experiences that promote feelings of special personal power, grandiosity, or egocentricity are likely to be the result of a threatened self-image seeking to re-establish its dominance over destiny. Common sense tells us that such occurrences reflect the need for deep affirmation or reassurance of one's valued, graced life in God—not affirmation of the experience, but affirmation of the person.

Vivid experiences of calling or direction (voices, visions, or senses that say "Do this" or "Don't do that") need to be examined carefully for any sense of grandiosity and for their real directional value in daily life. Such visions or callings may at first seem radical and surprising, but if legitimate, they will be borne out by circumstances. At the other end of the spectrum, feelings of emptiness, darkness, or alienation from God can be considered in terms of whether they represent primary psychological depression, internal resistance, or more clearly spiritual experiences of the "dark night of the senses." More will be said of this in Chapter 5.

The religiously oriented hallucinations, delusions, and preoccupations that occur so commonly in psychosis are usually quite obvious in their pathology. It takes no great psychiatric expertise to see that such phenomena are nearly always self-serving and compensatory, that they represent the efforts of a wounded, fragmented self-image to feel more special and powerful. Such phenomena generally cause a person to feel different from and in most cases better than other people, and they are nearly always associated with deterioration in other areas of life and functioning. Further, it is usually quite obvious that they are held with great attachment, with a tension and a rigidity that are obviously defensive in nature.

Extrasensory and parapsychological experiences need to be evaluated not so much on the basis of their actual validity or nature as in terms of how seriously one takes them. Precognitive or prophetic dreams and subtle telepathic senses are very common among the general population, in my experience, and do seem to be increasingly discovered, developed, or refined during the course of spiritual practice. Usually such experiences are more distressing than exciting for the individual because they provide extra information without any real guidelines as to how to use this information. How does one respond, for example, to a dream that seems to foretell trouble for someone else? Most people are wisely reluctant to dash off with every such dream to proclaim danger to the parties involved. Still, not to do anything in the face of such strong senses may feel like an abrogation of responsibility. It is often this sense of dubious responsibility that makes precognitive or telepathic information so uncomfortable. In most cases it seems that there is little or nothing that can be done with such information, and the opening of these avenues of perception feels much more like a curse than a blessing. It has been my experience that such perceptions do not occur as special events of dramatic significance, but rather as part of a generally increasing perceptiveness and sensitivity that affect one's overall ability to be of service to others. In other words, a few precognitive dreams may not be important in terms of the dreams themselves, but may reflect that the person is becoming more sensitive, empathetic, and generally capable of dealing with others at a more intimate level. To be sure, some strong precognitive feelings will need to be considered carefully and (if possible) discussed in spiritual direction regarding whether any action should be taken in response to them. Traditional discernment methods apply here, for it is the course of action, the *direction* to be followed, that is in question. But in general, extrasensory experiences simply constitute another source of information—information that must be processed in the same way one would process normal sensory data.

Similar consideration must be given to more specific and practical abilities that may be discovered during the course of spiritual growth. The appearance of a gift for spiritual healing, for example, does not mean that one should immediately hang up a shingle and go into business. Time, care, and patience are needed to discern the legitimacy and strength of such gifts, and to gain some sense of how the Lord might be calling them to use.

In all of these issues, it is most important that the occurrence of the phenomenon itself not cause so much consternation or excitement that careful, considered appraisals are bypassed. There is a great need for a kind of overall leveling of specialness here. Many exciting and dramatic experiences or apparent gifts are nothing other than devices employed by internal or external forces that seek to distract and derail us from our constancy towards God. Others are true gifts that have definitely called-for meanings and applications. We will not be able to see those meanings or applications if we are obsessed with the excitement of the phenomena themselves.

A helpful rule of thumb here is whenever a spiritual experience or the search for spiritual experiences becomes the overriding focus of attention, things have gone astray. Although spiritual journeys often begin in the context of experience, and although experiences constitute major vehicles of insight, growth, support, and service along the way, the goal of the journey can never legitimately be experience itself. The goal is beyond experience, and has to do with our actually becoming who God means us to be and doing what God means us to do. Experiences can sometimes be helpful means towards this end, and they can sometimes get in the way. But they are never the end in themselves.

Some fully valid spiritual experiences may be so shocking, revealing, beautiful, frightening, or exciting that one cannot help but be at least transiently absorbed with them. This concern and attention may be necessary to integrate or even to "recover" from a particularly dramatic experience. But, as with profound shocks in other aspects of life, one needs to incorporate them and move on. And even during the crisis itself, there needs to be some remaining sense of the constant liveliness of God beneath and within the drama.

The spiritual director's role is very important here. While a directee is caught up in the momentary emotional turmoil of responding to an experience, the director needs to maintain a sense of the larger perspective. The experience, however dramatic, is only one way in which God is working in the person's life, one of many ways that constitute a lifelong journey towards deeper reconciliation.

Preoccupation with experience-for-the-sake-of-experience can occur at any point along the spiritual journey. It is clearly most obvious early on, but years of practice and direction are by no means absolute protection. It is often at the more "mature" levels of spiritual practice that the most seductive experiences occur. It would be hoped that by the time these subtly diverting phenomena occur, one might have had enough background of experience to receive them lightly and respond to them without excessive fascination. But this is not always the case. None of us, directee or director, can afford to bask dully, trusting in the wealth of our experience. It is not our task to trust experience, but to trust God—and this requires that we stay awake.

Dreams

Some special note needs to be made of the role of dreams in spiritual direction, not because dreams necessarily constitute a special form of experience, but because they are of central interest to some modern schools of spiritual direction that are evolving. For Freud, dreams were the "royal road to the unconscious." For Jung they constituted much the same kind of pathway to the "objective psyche" or "collective unconscious." Jung called them "small hidden doors in the deepest and most intimate sanctum of the soul."[5]

Primarily as a result of Jung's emphasis, a number of modern authorities see dream work as an especially revealing process of discernment, a kind of "royal road to the spirit."[6] It seems to me that dreams can indeed be avenues into deep and hidden areas of ourselves, and that as such they can be a way of increasing our appreciation of certain deep and hidden aspects of God's work within us. But it must also be remembered that dreams are subject to as much (if not more) psychological mediation, alteration, and distortion as any other kind of experience. Their apparent richness in symbolism is demonstrative of this. As I have indicated, one of the problems that can be encountered here is that analysis of dream content can constitute a major distraction of its own if one becomes preoccupied with it. In a sense, dream material seems so "good," so rich in insight, that it can become a decidedly "bad" object of fascination.

For completeness' sake, it should be noted that not all psychiatric authorities agree with the symbolic importance of dreams. Beginning in 1977, for example, Harvard sleep researchers suggested that dreams were essentially the result of a rather random firing of large neurons in the brain stem that occurs normally during certain sleep cycles.[7] The actual imagery of dreams and their content are felt by these researchers to be the result of the brain trying to "make sense" of such random and disparate signals rather than its reflecting of deep psychic symbolism. These studies have prompted considerable debate within the psychiatric profession, debate that at this writing is far from resolved. If their hypothesis is correct, it would remove much of the symbolic "specialness" from the dream theories of Freud and Jung, but it would still not mean that working with one's dreams could not continue to be a helpful source of self-exploration. The associations one has to dreams may be highly revealing even if the dreams themselves fail to be so.

It seems to me that spiritual directors need to make careful, prayerful, judicious, and individual decisions about how much attention to give to dreams and how much encouragement to directees to work with dreams on their own. Some persons who are especially intrigued and curious about their inner psychic worlds risk self-absorption in dream exploration. Others who have very weak ego defenses may even experience some psychological decompensation if confronted with too much unconscious symbolism.[8] Still others who are overly defended and "out of touch" with their inner worlds may benefit greatly by dream exploration. Thus, although dreams may or may not be very "special" tools for spiritual discernment, one does need to discern how, when, and how much to focus on them.

On balance, it is important that people in spiritual direction be attentive to their dreams and able to discuss them freely in the direction relationship. As with visionary experiences, there is ample scriptural evidence of God sometimes using dreams as both direct and indirect vehicles of communication. Thus, dreams are at least as pertinent to spiritual direction as are all other forms of experience. God speaks to us, calls us, and moves us in many ways. We need to be open and receptive to all these ways, and we need to refrain from allowing our interest in one to obscure the others.

Dreams can be examined in many ways, from simply discussing and reflecting upon them to extensive note taking and "journaling." Most of the common ways focus on the symbolic content of dreams and the relevance of this content to daily life and spiritual growth. Before leaving this topic, I would like to mention that there is another way of dream exploration—one that can be used to focus more on the "separate reality" of the dream world. This approach has not, to my knowledge, yet appeared in Christian spiritual direction, but it has a substantial historic place in certain Oriental and American Indian spiritualities.[9] The purpose of this approach in spiritual formation is to help loosen one's attachment to frozen and preconceived images of what is "real" and what is not. The methods involve a development of "lucid dreaming," learning how to maintain a wakeful awareness and intentionality within dreams. Sometimes this is combined with a practice of viewing daily life as if it were a dream.

Some modern psychological approaches to lucid dreaming are being developed and promulgated at the present time, but many of these do so from a standpoint that is still primarily content-oriented and subject to great fascination. They see "waking up in your dreams" as a way of achieving more exciting and dramatic experiences, and sometimes as a way of garnering personal "spiritual" power. I suspect it will not be long before lucid dreaming begins to appear in the context of some modern schools of spiritual direction. My hope is that if this happens it will attend to the task of loosening our attachments to world-images and increasing our appreciation of God's mystery rather than becoming preoccupied with generating more experiences of personal entertainment or power.

4. Mind: Spirituality and Psychodynamics

As I have said, the real importance of spiritual experiences can be considered only in terms of how they change and affect our lives in relation to God, ourselves, and each other. In part, these changes depend upon how we integrate and respond to the experiences. In spiritual direction it is necessary to examine such effects and responses carefully, rather than focusing simply on the content of an experience. This can be facilitated by asking questions like Where did this experience seem to come from? What was going on in your mind at the time? What relationship did it seem to have with your prayer? Has your attitude changed as a result of this experience; is there anything different in your daily life? Has your prayer life changed? What does this experience say to you about your relationship to God and to other people? Has it in any way helped you be less selfish and more loving? Where do you see grace in what you have been through?

Questions such as these encourage not only a critical evaluation of the experience and its effects, but also a "placing" of the experience in the larger context of a person's overall spiritual journey. Such questions—and most of the rest of the interchanges that occur in spiritual direction—take place at a "conscious" level. This means that both director and directee are aware of what is happening in their dialogue; most of the messages being communicated are direct enough to be taken at face value; and what is said is generally what is meant.

There is, however, another level that is always active in human life. Here, in the "unconscious" dimension, underlying meanings and messages may be quite different from those that are evident on the surface. What appears to be one thing when taken at face value may be quite another if the full truth were known. While one might hope—and I think justifiably expect—that spiritual direction relationships would be more transparent and less covert than other daily interactions, this can never be absolute. As we shall discuss in Chapter 6, many things can go on in spiritual direction of which both director and directee are totally unaware. More important at this point, however, is the fact that there is much of which we are unaware in our personal reactions and responses to God.

The Unconscious

Freud's most basic contribution to psychological understanding was his scientific demonstration that the unconscious dimension of mind does indeed exist. Before Freud there was almost no notion whatsoever that the human mind had a life beyond immediate awareness. Through his analyses of dreams, slips of the tongue, free association, and other phenomena, Freud demonstrated that in fact the majority of psychic activity occurs unconsciously. Jung expanded on Freud's individual observations and developed a concept of the "collective unconscious" or "objective psyche," a vast psychic groundwork shared by all humanity.

Freud saw human mental functioning as taking place within three arenas: the *conscious,* that small field of which a person can be immediately aware at any given time; the *preconscious,* a larger reservoir from which memories can come readily into awareness; and the *unconscious,* the largest and most inaccessible realm. This system of understanding still holds up well today from a psychodynamic standpoint, as long as these arenas are recognized as qualities of mental function rather than actual entities or places within the brain.

Freud's work with dreams is illuminating in terms of a full understanding of this schema. While it is occurring, a dream takes place consciously; one is aware of it at the time. Most dreams slip from immediate awareness into memory shortly after we awaken. Many of these, however, can be recalled if we put a little effort into it. These can be said to have moved into the preconscious realm and then back into the conscious when they are remembered.

Some dreams cannot be remembered at all. These have been fully "repressed," moved from conscious to unconscious levels.

Further, conscious and unconscious psychic activity can be identified within the dream itself. The images, experiences, and sensations that occur within the dream are called its *manifest content*. These are conscious, at least at the time of the dream. According to standard psychodynamic theory, other, deeper meanings of the dream are unconscious and are expressed or reflected only through the symbolism of the manifest dream content. These underlying meanings are called the *latent content*. For example, someone may dream of cleaning and refurbishing a dirty, run-down house (manifest content) that might symbolize an unconscious desire to be rid of ugly or destructive impulses and to create a new attitude towards life (latent content).

A case can be made—and was taken to extremes at some points in the Freudian era—that all human activity is comprised of latent as well as manifest content. It is out of this assumption that a host of psychiatric jokes arose, from the psychiatrist saying "I wonder what he meant by that" after someone says "Hello," to the classic "Why can't a cigar just be a cigar?" In modern times one can be safe in assuming that a good number of human experiences are probably just what they seem to be—no hidden meanings. But at the same time, many experiences do have unconscious symbolic content. Even more importantly, conscious desires and aspirations may be blocked because of unconscious resistances and defenses. The spiritual arena is by no means an exception to this. In fact, it is within spiritual activity that one may encounter the most subtle and convoluted kinds of unconscious resistances.

For years, a large number of people have believed that "the unconscious" represents the deepest and most profound level of being. But when spiritual matters are acknowledged, one must consider still deeper dimensions. The difference is that these levels are not only "deeper," but also more transcendent. They are no longer precisely within our individual or collective psyches. They are beyond us and yet they reflect the ground in which our being is rooted.

When one fully acknowledges this transcendent dimension of reality, it becomes obvious that the plumbing of psychic depths does not necessarily constitute the primary path to God. It may be one avenue of exploration, but only one of many. Self-understanding most assuredly can aid and foster one's appreciation of the divine, but as I have indicated earlier, the divine is certainly not to be found entirely within ourselves or within our race. We are marvelously incarnated creations, but around us there exists a whole universe of other marvelous creations, of space, form, and energy. At the root of *all* of this is the Creator. We may be very specially loved in God's heart, but we are not alone there.

In Chapter 2 I mentioned that our own fears and resistances constitute one of the four major forces impinging upon our growth in spirit. Now, we must also understand that many of these fears and resistances occur at an unconscious level. In the course of spiritual growth, especially if competent direction is available, we may become increasingly aware of these unconscious psychological forces. In other words, experiences of resistance or defensiveness against spiritual insight can be brought into awareness, apprehended, and understood as a result of prolonged experience in prayer and spiritual direction. This is not too much unlike the classic psychotherapeutic process in which unconscious psychodynamics that have impeded life-efficiency are brought to light and thereby lose some of their power.

Two examples for comparison may help in understanding this. An interchange in a very stereotyped and condensed psychotherapeutic situation might go as follows:

Patient: I tried to make some notes about my dreams as you suggested last week, but I can't seem to be able to do it. The strangest thing is happening. I put a pencil and paper by my bed before I go to sleep, but in the morning when I wake up I forget to make any notes. I get up, take my shower, and get dressed, and *then* I remember what I was supposed to do. But by then I've forgotten all my dreams. I guess I just need more self-discipline if I'm going to do this correctly.

Therapist: So you really want to do it but you keep forgetting. . . . Do you suppose there might be some reason for forgetting, some resistance? Some part of you that really *doesn't* want to do it?

Patient [*reflecting quietly*]: I guess there must be . . . but I can't think of anything. . . . Maybe I'm dreaming things I really don't want to know . . . but it's happening every day, every single day since you told me to do it . . . I don't know. . . . I remembered a lot of dreams without having to take notes before this past week, but ever since you told me to make the notes I haven't remembered a single one. . . . Sometimes it seems I can't do anything right. . . . This is beginning to depress me.

Therapist: Any memories of similar kinds of feelings in the past?

Patient: Yeah, I was just thinking it's like the trouble I sometimes used to have with school assignments. . . . I'd know what the assignment was, but I'd totally forget to do it.

Therapist: Did this seem like an assignment to you?

Patient: Yes . . . well, it didn't seem that way last week when we talked about it. At that time it was just an idea we came up with that might help. But I sure did turn it into an assignment . . . and now there's all that garbage attached to it, like I've got to do it right to please you . . . or to get your approval. . . .

After this, the discussion might proceed to identify the patient's long-standing anger about having to do what parental figures ordered, and perhaps some other patterns of "passive-aggressive" resistance might come to light. But probably the interchange as described would be sufficient to remove the patient's specific blocks to recording dreams. Thus, a resistance of which the patient had been totally unaware has been brought more fully into awareness, and its power has thereby been diminished. Compare this with a dialogue that might take place in spiritual direction, again very stereotyped and condensed.

Directee: Do you remember how full of joy I was about my prayer the last time we talked? Well, to put it mildly, things have changed. Last month I was truly seeing myself as a child of God, not only when I prayed but also at many times during each day. I even felt that I was radiating some of God's warmth and love to others. But then it all just seemed to disappear.

Director: What is your prayer like now?

Directee [*laughing sarcastically*]: *What* prayer? Every time I sit down to pray my mind is filled with all the other things I should be doing. Many days I don't have time to pray at all . . . or at least I can't seem to take the time. . . .

Director: Well, if prayer is so unpleasant for you right now, it certainly makes sense that you would not be so willing to take the time for it.

Directee: Yes, but I do still *want* to. . . . God knows, I would give anything to have that joyful radiance again. It just doesn't seem right; is God so fickle that He just gives it and takes it away? Is that what all this "consolation and desolation" business is about? Is it some kind of test?

Director: Do you have any sense that God has withdrawn from you?

Directee [*pausing*]: I don't really think so. There have been some times when I felt that way, but now it's more like . . . uh, like there's something stuck in between me and God. [*Long silence*] . . . It's tough.

Director: What's tough?

Directee: Being a child of God. I mean you have to really give yourself, you have to sacrifice so much. It's worth it if you get that wonderful feeling of joy, but when nothing comes in return for it . . .

Director: Did it seem like a sacrifice when you were feeling so good about everything?

Directee: No. I felt like I was giving—no, it was more like God was giving Himself through me to others. No, it didn't seem like I was doing anything special . . . well, I did start giving at some point. I remember I was thinking "This is wonderful. . . . I can express God's love so fully. . . . I can do for others, be for others, a symbol of God's love." I suppose I started to *do* it more.

Director: Did it get to be too much? For a while you felt so close to God, and all that love was just coming through you, and then after a while maybe you started trying to do it yourself. Then perhaps it was a little less God and a little more you. Maybe it was too much, not to be *doing* anything *yourself*. It's possible that that's where the real sacrifice was, that you *weren't* doing it yourself.

Directee: That sounds right. I can feel myself relaxing as you talk. But it's crazy. There didn't seem to be any distress *until* I started trying to do it myself. Before that everything just flowed. I just flowed, the world just flowed, God just flowed through it all. It was so delicious. . . . It's crazy that I'd pull away from that. Yes, but I know I've always pulled away. That's the story of my life; I keep pulling away just when things start seeming perfect. That's the same old thing. I know what I need to do. I need to take a deep breath and relax again. . . . Oh, I don't *have* to do it all. . . .

From this point the discussion may or may not proceed to more clearly identify the threat to self-image posed by the directee's experience of being so close to God, and the precise ways in which that self-image had been re-asserted by trying-to-do instead of allowing. (See further comments about self-image threats on page 68.) Again, however, the interchange as described is probably sufficient to alleviate the immediate problem.

In both of these situations unconscious resistances had been subverting conscious desire and intentions, and the bringing to light of these resistances allowed movement forward. In neither case did the interchange constitute any kind of "cure." The patient's resistance to authority is very likely to recur in other ways, though with repeated identification and understanding it could probably be minimized. The directee's situation is certain to recur in a myriad of forms, no matter how many times it is identified or how well it is understood.

The major difference here is that while the patient's problem is a simple personality trait based on past experience, the directee is struggling with the very existence of self-image in the face of close appreciation of the divine. Unconsciously that self-image is engaged in a life-or-death battle, and although all conscious intents may be in the direction of spiritual surrender and dying-to-self, a host of unconscious defenses will be brought to bear in order to preserve, bolster, and re-assert that image of self. Further, the directee's situation is one that is shared by all people. Everyone will resist surrendering attachment to the importance of self-image. Thus, while the patient is expressing an individual—albeit not uncommon—problem, the directee is expressing a universally human condition.

This distinction is especially important in terms of the role of the helper in such situations. It is the function of therapists to help patients solve problems. But although spiritual directors may also be called upon to help solve various problems (such as blocks to prayer or obstacles to realization) their most fundamental role is to attend to God's power, love, and grace in the directee's situation. Thus, while psychological knowledge can be very helpful for spiritual directors, the thing that really counts is the directors' graced capacity to intend and attend towards God. They must not allow their concern for problem solving to cloud their perceptions of what God may be calling for in the overall life-process of their directees.

The Unconscious and Pathology

The process of human spiritual growth is impinged upon by unconscious forces in a multiplicity of ways. Not all of these unconscious forces act against spiritual growth. As a matter of fact, the very heart of our longing for God often remains unconscious until the time is right for it to emerge. For example, it is not uncommon for people to feel a subtle uneasiness in the midst of a life that otherwise seems filled with satisfaction. All one's basic needs may be met and all one's relationships going well, yet there may be a deep inner nagging, a longing for something more or something different that might make life truly complete. I feel that regardless of the context in which it may be submerged, this uneasiness represents the barest edge of our hunger for God, surfacing in awareness as little more than a nudge that we do not understand. Years or even decades may pass before this nudge turns into an identifiable spiritual longing. Sometimes it is never so identified. The timing of its birth into full awareness is, I think, something that no human being can engineer. We are not wise enough to know when it should happen, and our hands are too clumsy to force it to happen truthfully and healthfully. We can only attempt to foster the kinds of settings and atmospheres around ourselves and each other that will not impede its unfolding.

Most importantly, we need to refrain from any attempt to label this deep and subtle uneasiness as pathological. In the absence of clearly identifiable disorder, it is terribly destructive to encourage the dulling or denial of this deepest existential discomfort, for this is one pain we are not meant to anesthetize ourselves to; one hunger we are not meant to deny; one "problem" we are not meant to fix with our own hands. Yet millions of us attempt to do this daily. We seek to ease our longing for love and union through furtive, passing intensities with each other. We take our existential distress to therapy assuming we can remedy it if we learn how to live correctly. We seek our deepest meaning in what we can achieve through the work of our own hands. Even more often we kill our inner longing by dulling our awareness with tranquilizers, alcohol, food, work, and the host of behavioral sedations that we falsely call recreation. True recreation, like true rest, leaves us with greater energy and clearer awareness. But when we narcotize ourselves, regardless of the means, we are left clouded and sapped of strength.

This habit of dulling ourselves to escape from uneasiness is so ingrained that I doubt we can ever overcome it entirely. But we do not need to encourage it in ourselves or in others. We do not need to do any more of it than we have to. In this, it may be helpful simply to remember that our most basic dis-ease may not be a disorder at all. Instead, it may be our finest hope.

In classic spiritual direction it is traditional for directors to help directees evaluate sufferings and discomforts in terms of their graced potentials. Certainly this approach is far more likely to happen in spiritual direction than in counseling or psychotherapy, which nearly always leap to "remedy the problem." But in the midst of our modern problem-solving mentality, spiritual directors are too often seduced into simplistic attempts to make their directees feel better. We must reclaim some of the old wisdom that says there is a difference between consolation and simply feeling good, and that suffering is often indeed the outer clothing of growth. This is not of course a call back to old puritanical notions that suffering is always good for the soul or that something is always wrong with feeling good. There is usually little need to seek out any additional suffering. If one does not run away or dull oneself to the suffering naturally given in life, it will be sufficient.

If we are truly open to the Spirit's potential, we will be able to acknowledge that pain and pleasure, joy and sadness, success and failure—all these things may work either for or against our growth in spirit. Similarly, the fact that a given desire or feeling is unconscious does not mean it will work against us, just as our conscious desires and feelings do not always work for us. In the discussions that follow, then, it will be important to understand three things:

1. All experienced phenomena can be expected to have at least some connections with unconscious psychodynamics.
2. These connections are neither good nor bad in and of themselves. It is only upon considering their fruits—their effects upon the experienced and lived life of faith—that one can begin to appreciate and appraise their true value.
3. Even if a given phenomenon is determined to be destructive, this does not mean it cannot in some way include a deeply graced dimension. God can speak to us in destruction as well as in creation.

Psychological Preconditioning in Spiritual Growth

Closely allied with the concept of the unconscious is the traditional assertion that all people carry with them strong psychological determinants from their early childhood years. So strong are these early experiences and patternings that basic personality is often said to be essentially established by the age of six. While there is always room for change, there is also no doubt that the habitual ways we relate to the world have been strongly preconditioned. We carry with us basic attitudes of trusting or mistrusting, fundamental self-appraisals of value or worthlessness, and deep-seated fears, aspirations, longings, and revulsions that are our heritage from childhood. In pop-psychological jargon these old determinants are called tapes, programs, or scripts. In religious circles the term baggage is often used to refer to old negative experiences related to childhood, parents, and church.

There is a difference of opinion among behavioral scientists as to how changeable these patterns might be. Some say that the human mind is so flexible that it can alter any aspect of itself if given sufficient technology and motivation. Some would even maintain that genetic determinants like basic activity level and intellectual capacity can be modified. Others, however, feel that the only valid approach to human psychology is to help people make the best of what they have been given. Even within theological circles there is some room for debate concerning how deeply open to change human beings can be. Most Christian thought includes a belief that the Power of the Holy Spirit can radically transform anyone, that people can truly be born again and re-created. Still, there is some scriptural basis for a case to be made that some people are inherently much more open to (or selected for) such change than others.[1]

In spiritual direction, however, there has to be an ongoing awareness that anything can happen; that the Holy Spirit is already affecting the person; and that one must participate in this work through careful discernment and support. Here again, it is necessary to walk the fierce path of free will and dependence. We must always claim the freedom we have been given, to do otherwise would devalue our humanity. But at the same time, we will increasingly recognize the extreme inadequacy of personal will and knowledge in figuring out what life is or how we should live it. As we grow in wisdom, we also grow in the realization of our utter dependence upon the Lord in all things. It seems to me, then, that in its purest human form spiritual direction is a journey towards more freely and deeply choosing to surrender to God.

In the course of this journey it is inevitable that one will encounter many old preconceptions, conditionings, and other pieces of baggage that affect one's willingness towards God. Usually the greatest emphasis is placed upon those factors that seem to impede one's growth. But as I have stated, not all preconditionings are negative. Some may be very helpful and supportive for later spiritual growth. To minimize the modern medical mind-set that always seeks solutions to problems, it is important to pay some attention to the positive, growth-promoting qualities that exist in past experiences. Even more importantly, one must remember that although we may be able to distinguish health and strength from pathology and weakness according to our own values, we are simply not wise enough to know the difference in any ultimate sense. What may seem to us a severe weakness or incapacity may turn out to be a great strength when all the spiritual data are in. One would do well to remember the beatitudes in this regard. Baggage can wear us down and impede us, but it can also contain some very helpful items for our journeys. Keeping this in mind, we may consider a few examples of preconditionings that affect spiritual growth.

Basic Trust and Mistrust

These terms, coined by Erik Erikson, refer to extremely early experiences in meeting life and handling tasks.[2] If very primitive tasks—as fundamental as finding the nipple with the mouth—are successful, basic trust builds. Lack of success in such tasks breeds basic mistrust. These early experiences, according to Erikson, lead to attitudes that color the rest of life. At this level of development, basic trust and mistrust do not necessarily apply to "self" versus "others." Only later do they take on such specific objects. Underneath, they remain fundamental, unattached attitudes. If one, then, has a preponderance of basic trust, most situations in life will be met with a sense that "things are going to be all right" or "everything will work out for the best." If basic mistrust predominates, one is likely to approach life looking for all the dangers and threats that might exist, and to expect negative results from any enterprise.

In simplistic terms, these attitudes constitute a kind of existential optimism/pessimism balance pertaining to the overall thrust of one's endeavors and encounters.

It is likely—though not always certain—that basic trust and mistrust will affect the spiritual journey as much as they affect the rest of one's life. If one tends to mistrust oneself and others in school, work, and social relationships, a similiar attitude will likely be carried into prayer. Here one might assume that basic trust is always an aid and mistrust always an impediment to spiritual growth. While this is probably true as long as one relates to specific images of a God who is circumscribed and wholly "other," it is also possible that the inability to trust in such objects and in one's own abilities may lead to deep existential despair. In turn, this despair can sometimes be the very doorway to hope. Not trusting in any identifiable thing, it is sometimes possible to offer everything to the unknowable mystery of God beyond all things, to give up everything, to surrender all of oneself because there simply is no option other than suicide. This existential extremity does not occur very often, for it represents not the penultimate choice of suicide-or-continuing-to-struggle, but the ultimate precipice of suicide-or-surrender.

Similarly, a high degree of basic trust does not always ensure steady spiritual growth. Extremes of basic trust can lead to destructive gullibilities, misplaced surrenders, and false beliefs in one's own ability to master destiny. It seems to me that in spite of its pathologic connotations, basic mistrust—at least in small doses—might just carry a bit of sanity with it. However one may feel about the essential "healthiness" of basic trust or mistrust, it is important to remember that although these qualities may precondition many aspects of spiritual growth, they do not *predetermine* either the course or the outcome of that growth. As always, grace is ever capable of surprising us.

Preconceptions of Self-Image

Nearly all theorists of personality development hold that the establishment of self-image is one of the most important processes of childhood. The image we have of ourselves—one component of "identity"—deeply affects how we meet the world and the attitudes with which we encounter images of God. At the outset it should be understood that one's image of self is no more real than one's image of God. We are at core endlessly mysterious, and our self-images are simply expedient symbols of who we really are. This is, of course, also true for our images of God.

Thus the meeting between self-image and God-image is just that—a meeting of images. Contemplative experience makes it obvious that the "real" meeting is quite different—so different, in fact, that words cannot describe it. Here one mystery finds its ground in the eternal mystery of the Creator of all mysteries. It is at this level, I assume, that we are truly made in the image of God.

Images of both self and God are necessary as symbols. Without them we could not speak, think, nor intend. Thus, the way in which self-image is construed during childhood is bound to affect our later sense of relationship to God. Three aspects of self-image are especially important in this regard: the basic strength of self-image, its quality, and its importance.

1. Strength of Self-Image

The prevailing cultural attitude of the modern West is that self-image should be as strong as possible. Most children are taught from a very early age that the way to get along in life is to stand up for themselves; to know who they are and what they want out of life and how to get it; to establish themselves as solid, autonomous beings. Since this teaching usually occurs while a child is dependent upon parents and must follow the orders of authorities, the lesson is hard to learn. Some children are forced into ravages of self-doubt simply because their parents push them so hard to be self-determining. Others don't receive enough opportunity to test the limits of their autonomy. Because of both such extremes, many people find upon reaching adulthood that they must go through further processes of individualization in order to achieve the degree of autonomy mandated by society.[3] To accomplish this, they may turn to psychotherapy, assertiveness training, or a host of other self-help modalities.

It is often not until after one has spent the better part of one's life seeking autonomy and self-determination that spiritual awakening occurs, and then it seems one is called upon to reverse the process. Now what is needed is not heroic mastery but the simplicity of becoming as a little child; not self-determination but self-surrender; not self-assertion but dying-to-self. But by this time the thrust towards establishing and maintaining strength of self-image is usually so ingrained that it continually confounds one's intentions towards spiritual surrender. In all people there are inherent forces that fight such profound surrender, forces that are bolstered and supported by incredibly powerful prevailing norms in our culture. It is easy to understand why people so frequently think of "running off to a monastery" to pursue their intentional spiritual journeys. An internal monastery is very difficult to establish in a culture that is constantly subverting surrender.

Thus, the strength of self-image impinges very directly upon one's reactions to spiritual experiences. If my self-image is dependent upon what I can control or how much power I have, then experiences of surrender or humility in the face of God will be exceedingly threatening. If my self-image depends upon what I can do, then the silence and passive receptiveness of open prayer may prove extremely difficult. If my self-image depends upon strict maintenance of self/other boundaries, I may emphatically deny and actively avoid unitive experiences. Even experiences of deep belonging may be accompanied by considerable anxiety. The hard fact of the matter is that our self-images do depend upon all of these things.

For the person who has established a strong self-image, experiences of surrender, silence, and union constitute threats to the maintenance of the status quo. They represent changes so radical and incomprehensible that one cannot help but resist them. Here, the heart knows that spiritual surrender and a realization of basic rootedness in God are what is most deeply desired, but the mind has been trained to believe that this is just not the way things are supposed to be. The result is usually an attempt to distort both factors to come up with some contrived arrangement for having the cake and eating it too, an arrangement in which some sense of God can be subsumed without having to sacrifice personal mastery. The person described early in this chapter who began to take over the "doing" of God's love was encountering this kind of distortion. Spiritual pride and spiritual narcissism are other examples (see pages 82–83).

For the person who has not established a strong self-image, the person whose sense of personal power and control is *weak* or whose ego-boundaries are fragmentary, the threat of spiritual experiences may be even greater. Such experiences may be reminiscent of troubling past events, of feeling powerless and devastated by other people. Here again the heart may know what is wanted, but the mind is bound to resist. In this case. the compromise may take the form of contriving to make God a part of one's self-image, an artificial substitute for personal inadequacies. The most extreme examples of this are, of course, those psychotic delusions in which a person comes to believe that he or she is God or Jesus, or has been especially chosen by God to carry out some grandiose mission (the nature of which is, of course, determined by the person's own inner needs). As another example, people with weak self-images may feel that God is constantly leading them into catastrophes, when in fact they themselves are clearly engineering the catastrophes.

Thus strong self-images may contrive an artificial union with God, and weak self-images may incorporate a contrived God. I believe that if the matter of spiritual growth were in our hands alone, these tendencies towards distortion and artificiality would absolutely prevent us from any progress. However noble or accurate our conscious intent may be, our minds would always be capable of subverting the desires of our hearts. It is our only hope for salvation, I feel, that our search for God is seeded, borne, supported, and accompanied by God's search for us.[4]

2. *Quality of Self-Image*

The strength and the quality of self-image are essentially unrelated. "Strength" implies the stability of one's self-definition, "quality" refers to the evaluation one has of oneself—whether I am basically good or bad, worthy or unworthy, lovable or contemptible, adequate or inadequate. An individual may feel unworthy, inadequate, and contemptible, but this implies only that the quality of self-image is negative, not that the image itself is weak. If these evaluations are held firmly and consistently, the self-image is just as strong as that of a person who believes firmly and consistently in his or her own merit and goodness.

A very weak self-image vacillates between extremes of self-degradation and grandiosity depending upon life circumstances and upon approval or rejection by other people. A very strong self-image holds to its preconceived self-evaluations, good or bad, regardless of external circumstances. From the standpoint of spiritual growth, at least, one could pose that there are advantages and disadvantages to both. Strong self-images may be more determined and self-fulfilling in their enterprises toward God, but they are also more rigid and less open to surrender. Weak self-images may surrender more readily and be generally more open, but their surrenders are easily misplaced and they are more readily swayed by extraneous circumstances.

In terms of the qualities of self-image, people who have grown up with very positive self-appraisals—those who as children were repeatedly affirmed as being good and worthwhile—often have an easier time of relating to their images of God, at least as long as those images continue to be of a God who is primarily "other." They are more likely to see themselves as worthy of God's love than are those with negative self-images. They more readily accept the notion that they are forgiven, and they have a greater optimism and energetic enthusiasm in their spiritual searching. In contrast, people with negative self-images are likely to have to struggle with feelings of being unlovable or unworthy of God's grace. Even if one believes that God has offered forgiveness, it may remain impossible to forgive oneself. And seeing oneself as a chronic failure makes it difficult to produce much enthusiasm or endurance in spiritual practice.

From the opposite viewpoint, people with positive self-images may be less likely to feel and to respond to their own internal longings for God. It is much easier for them to substitute personal success and interpersonal affirmations for their more basic spiritual hungers. Those with negative self-images may be more likely to feel that God is their only hope for fulfillment. They tend to seek the real thing—something that is beyond themselves as well as within; something different from their images of themselves; something that carries the hope of reconciliation and rebirth.

3. Importance of Self-Image

It can be seen that a simple estimation of the strength or quality of self-image will not suffice as a predictor of how one may progress in the course of spiritual growth. The importance of self-image, however, makes more of a difference. Importance refers to how seriously one takes oneself, how much of one's time and energy is spent in activities that serve to maintain, bolster, perpetuate, or otherwise address one's feelings about oneself. Self-importance has a decidedly narcissistic quality, a self-centeredness that influences nearly all one's activities.

When self-image is very important one may appear openly self-ish, seeking in all things to come out on top, to be the leader, to serve one's own interests. Or the self-centeredness may be more covert, cloaked in the guise of altruism and concern for others. Here the narcissism can be detected only by revealing that underly-ing motivations are self-serving, that one is, for example, doing charitable acts not simply because they need to be done, but be-cause by doing them one builds or re-establishes one's own good feelings.

It is commonly assumed that such self-centeredness or self-importance is the result of a weak and/or negative self-image, but this is not always the case. One can easily recognize when grandio-sity is a compensation for feelings of inadequacy, but there are some people who have very strong, positive self-images who remain self-important simply because they consistently see the world only in terms of themselves. By early instruction and long-ingrained habit, they feel very good and confident and solid in themselves, yet are motivated only by their own desires and self-interest. This kind of orientation was described by Freud as the narcissistic personal-ity.[5] Freud felt this type of personality was characteristic of many people who became national or world leaders. He saw this as an especially valuable adjustment for leaders, because such people are not easily swayed by the opinions of others.

From a spiritual standpoint, self-importance can be understood as attachment to self-image.[6] As such, self-importance probably constitutes the single most difficult psychological obstacle to spiri-tual growth. The more one is attached to one's image of oneself, the more resistance one will have to its surrender. The more one sees the world through the eyes and perspective of self-image, the more difficult it will be to begin to see God's reality in the world. This is true regardless of the psychological origins of self-

importance. I may be very attached to my self-image because I feel
inadequate and worthless, because my image is so negative. In contrast, you may be very attached to your self-image because it is so
good, because it gives you so much pleasure and gratification. Still
another person may be very attached to self-image simply out of
habit or because the culture teaches us to be thus attached. Regardless of our motivations, all of us who are attached to self-image will
be having considerable difficulty with spiritual growth, because
spiritual growth inevitably leads towards a lessening of attachment
in general, and this includes most importantly a lessening of attachment to self-image.

Attachment to self-image is more a product of the human condition than a symptom of specific psychodynamic problems. We are
all prey to it in greater or lesser degree. It may take many forms
and be associated with a variety of psychological nuances, but attachment to self-image constitutes one of the most basic battle-
grounds of true spiritual searching. If in this battle spiritual
growth is to win out over psychological resistance, attachment to
self-image must—through grace—be lessened. The first stage of
this involves questions like Do I live for myself or for God? or Am
I seeking to do God's will or my own? Later on, it may become
Am I me or am I an expression of God? Finally it is simple, word-
less surrender and acceptance of grace. At this point, the conflict of
self-vs.-God no longer exists, because self-image has ceased to be
important. To phrase this more precisely, one might say that self-
image has lost its importance while the soul, the true reality of
one's being *behind* all images, accepts a devastatingly radical and
revolutionary new importance in responding to grace. Positive and
negative self-judgments, personal successes and failures, territories
and boundaries of self and other, all these things that had been
used to perpetuate self-concern lose their ultimate existential significance. They become nothing more than paper-thin symbols of
our endlessly mysterious true nature that is so deeply loved *by,*
important *to,* and made in the image *of,* God.

Few if any of us ever remain for long in this ideal state. Yet we
have all experienced tastes of it on numerous occasions in our lives.
And we have encountered other people who at least temporarily
have reflected it for us. These experiences constitute one of the

major sources of our personal spiritual motivation. At some level—unconscious, preconscious, or conscious—there is always within us the promise and the hope of being released from the bonds of attachment to self-image and being freed to be fully the children of God that we are.

Early Symbols and Images of God

Images of God that are planted in early childhood constitute another example of psychological preconditioning. Children are taught certain things about the nature of God at a very early age. Many of these teachings prove to be immensely helpful and provide a sound basis for later development, but many are also confusing and lead to distortion.

Some parents who use a God-image to help maintain discipline and control portray God as a stern judge, a severe taskmaster who keeps an ongoing tally of the child's deeds and misdeeds. Obviously this may instill an inordinate fear of God and may limit or actually prevent an appreciation of God's love and forgiveness. Other parents, perhaps in an attempt to prevent such harshness, may present God only as Love and avoid all anthropomorphism. For little children, this is often too abstract to deal with or to integrate in a meaningful way. It may preserve the mystery of God for children, but it does not really give them anyone to pray to. In most such cases, children invent their own conscious and unconscious images of God, based on some composite of people they have known and attributes of God they have heard about elsewhere.

Regardless of what images are presented by parents, most young children develop a sense of God as being active in their lives. They see God as a person or a force that influences their daily activities, brings good things or abandons them to bad things, and they attempt to appease God in much the same way that primitive religions do—or as we sophisticated adults do when we are truly frightened or despairing.[7]

Children are also strongly influenced by books, movies, and television in developing and refining images of God. Many are exposed to differing religious traditions and values in this way. Thus their images may often be more sophisticated and flexible than those of earlier generations who did not have the benefits and curses of such a media onslaught. One young boy said that God was like "the Force" referred to in the *Star Wars* movies. Another saw God as an ultimate superhero who had not yet made it to the Saturday morning cartoon schedule.

While considerable attention can be given to these overt ("manifest") God-images, we must be especially cognizant of the qualities of image that form unconsciously, the "latent" elements. These are often experienced only as hints of feelings when a child attempts to pray or to reflect upon God, but they carry great weight in terms of later experience. In addition, these underlying qualities may remain unchanged and continually active while our conscious images of God mature and become more sophisticated. The image of God as "Father," for example, is inevitably influenced by the child's human father. An image of God as powerful may be associated with dominance and submission issues and with dependency conflicts or competitive strivings. Here, it is not so much what the child is overtly taught about the nature of God that counts, but the way different words and experiences connect symbolically.

For example, a young woman said that while Jesus seemed a very real person to her, she had never felt she could get close to him. In clarifying this, she said that she had an internal sense of Jesus being intimately close, but whenever she thought about him or had any image of him it seemed she always had to keep her distance. In a much later discussion of a seemingly unrelated matter, she suddenly laughed and said:

I know why I can't get close to Jesus; it's because he has bad breath! You know how in Sunday School—gee, I must have been maybe four or five at the time—we'd sit in this little circle on the floor and sing "Jesus Loves Me." The first memory I have of that song was about the verse that goes "We are weak but he is strong." Well, I remember feeling this real yukky sensation about that word "strong." And just now I made a connection. My father had been eating an onion—it must have been the same day or the day before we sang that song in Sunday school—and he was remarking about how "strong" the onion was, and his breath was just atrocious. And then that word came up in the song . . . all I could think of was that horrible smell.

It should be noted before proceeding that this previously unconscious aspect of the image of Jesus had not interfered with the woman's heartfelt sense of relationship with Jesus. It only impeded her visual imagery and imaginative thinking about relating to Jesus. It would not be expected that spiritual direction should ferret out all such aberrations and resolve them; there are so many in each of us that to attempt this would prove an endless undertaking. Spiritual direction should, whenever possible, focus on that heartfelt sense beneath the imagery, and deal with minor image-distortions only when they can be identified as causing real problems. In other words, the realization that some image-distortions exist should not cause one to immediately embark on a crusade to correct them all.

It is obvious that images of the divine are every bit as subject to distortion and psychodynamic influence during personality development as are our images of ourselves. Simple associations of words, experiences, and sensations can condense upon and affect image-formation in a variety of ways. Similarly, people and things may become substitutes for images of God. One man said that he had always sensed God as a mixture of white cloth, brown wood, and golden metal because these were the perceptions he had of the altar in church as a small boy.

As has been emphasized before, our images of God are certainly not God; we must expect that with personal maturation as well as spiritual growth, some images of God will die and be replaced by others more "mature," while some images will remain deep within us, unchanging, yet affecting our experience. Given the mysterious nature of human psychic development, I doubt there is much we can do to prevent distortions of God- and self-images in our children. My personal sense, though, is that some of these distortions might be minimized if we could look upon the growth of our children a little more as a graced process of the Spirit's work within them and a little less as the product of our own manipulations of them.

Childhood Experiences

While relationship of self-image to God-image may be an intriguing arena for psycho-religious exploration, one must seek still deeper levels for a more accurate vision of human spirituality. One of these involves experiences one has had that are reminiscent of the experiences of spiritual growth. Here I refer to early experiences that may be associated with spiritually loaded qualities such as surrender, loss of control, being in a subservient relationship to authority, being quiet and still, sensing the cessation of thoughts, or noticing substantial changes in the quality of awareness. These have much more impact on later experience and spiritual practice than do simple image-formations, and are more likely to need addressing in spiritual direction.

Most people, for example, feel very ambivalent about the whole notion of spiritual surrender. While we all long at some level to relinquish our struggles for mastery and ache to rest in the loving peace of God, we are also terrified of what this kind of surrender might mean. It feels too much like dying. While this is a root-condition surpassing in influence both culture and individual personality formation, experiences of early childhood can either compound or alleviate the situation to some extent. One man experienced severe anxiety at the very thought of surrender or easing control. He readily spoke of several childhood experiences in which he had been severely abused by his father, and how he had learned to avoid these abuses by keeping a constant appearance of self-possession and competence.

Every time I let down my guard and allowed myself to appear the least bit vulnerable, my father would get me. If he didn't attack me with his fists, he would degrade and abase me with words. How am I to let go of my controls now with that kind of experience in my past?

In contrast, a woman described how peaceful and reassuring it was for her to surrender in prayer, and how in fact she often had to pull herself "back" into the activities of daily life with a good deal of effort. Her childhood experience was very relevant to this. She described both parents as loving, reliable, and consistently available to hold and reassure her whenever life seemed too difficult.

I guess it was easy for me—maybe a little *too* easy—to take a break from life and rest in my parents' arms. And it's even more easy to rest in the arms of God. God is always with me. I don't have to go home to find reassurance and rest. I can simply go home to God in my heart.

In the first instance, the man had to struggle with great fear even to relax in prayer. It helped him to understand how this was related to his past experience with his father, but his struggle remained monumental. In the second case, the woman had trouble going beyond the notion of just resting in God. She sometimes tended to use this resting as an escape from responsibilities. The man had difficulty accepting God's peace and reassurance because of his addiction to action. The woman had difficulty accepting that God's peace and reassurance always have implications *for* action.

As mentioned before, many people find their experiences in prayer colored by prior experiences with their father. The prevailing image of God as a masculine parent makes this impossible to avoid. As a result women sometimes find themselves with ambivalent feelings towards God or Jesus, and men sometimes struggle with competitive strivings or homosexual fears. Both sexes often have trouble accepting and integrating the maternal qualities of God. According to Jung, each man has within himself a female archetype (symbolic energy field) called *anima*. Similarly, a male archetype called *animus* resides within the psyche of each woman. Jung felt that growth towards wholeness ("individuation") implies an acceptance and integration of these opposite-sex archetypes. If true, this further complicates any human attempt to deal with an image of God that is distinctly masculine.

Even if one's personal prayer life and theology have transcended the restrictiveness of all the male pronouns used in referring to God, hearing them repeated in institutional contexts can still be a source of considerable turmoil and distraction. These difficulties almost invariably go deeper than simple image-associations. The emphasis on God's masculine authority stimulates unconscious remembrances of early male-dominance experiences for both sexes in our culture, and every time this happens it triggers a surge of ambivalence.

Sitting still in silence may also carry baggage from the past. A middle-aged man who found himself constantly restless and ill at ease in quiet prayer initially decided that he was "just not cut out to be a contemplative." Later however, he found that he could sit still, at least for short periods, if he gave himself permission to get up and walk around whenever he felt he needed to. Later yet, he recalled that as a child he had often been punished by being forced to sit still on a stool for up to an hour at a time. During his entire childhood, the only times he could remember sitting still and not doing anything were those times when he was being punished. In his case, this realization helped considerably. By consciously and intentionally reminding himself that to sit in quiet prayer was a free choice he himself made, his restlessness abated markedly.

Experiences such as radically changed awareness or stillness of mind that are so common in contemplative practice may also be affected by previous life-experiences. A man who had once come close to drowning later experienced trouble breathing whenever he felt his normal focus of attention expanding and quieting in prayer. Another man felt terrified whenever the number of thoughts in his mind started to decrease, he recalled a similar sensation as a teenager when undergoing anesthesia after a severe auto accident.

These are but a few examples of the ways in which life and prayer experience can be affected by earlier experiences that have qualities or attributes similar to those encountered in spiritual practice. In keeping with the pathology-focused "psychiatric" orientation here, I have emphasized the problematic aspects of such experiences. It should, however, be kept in mind that most early experiences can probably be seen as helpful and supportive to future spiritual growth, and even those with obviously distorting effects may have edges and dimensions that are constructive.

Pre-Existing Mind-Sets

The course of spiritual growth immerses one in a variety of new experiences. Images of reality are subject to dramatic change. What may have seemed at one time a coherently structured reality with clear subject/object distinctions and obvious differences between good and bad may now become very shuffled and shaken. One's usual bearings may disappear or become blurred, and the things one thought were known may become unknown. Subtle intuitive senses and delicate perceptions that once were hardly noticed may now take on more importance than any other form of information. What used to be expressible in words can become totally beyond comprehension, and words that previously held no meaning at all might suddenly become rich and full of life.

Early childhood conditioning may make a big difference in how readily one adapts to these kinds of changes. People who grew up in homes that emphasized strict adherence to specific ways of living may find it more difficult to acknowledge radical differences in perception. Or the opposite may be true; one may have felt so restricted by such rigidity that being without the usual structure may feel like a long sought-after freedom.

Many people were cautioned as children not to "think too much" or to go too deeply into spiritual matters, lest they should lose their faith or drive themselves crazy. In other homes, the whole arena of world views and religious beliefs may have been open for constant debate. Each of these orientations leaves its marks upon the children growing up therein. Thus, some people enter spiritual direction with very open minds and flexible world views; they may be more accepting of radical experience but at the same time have difficulty seeing it within the context of a given religious tradition. Others may be rooted in a tradition but rigidly resistant to and threatened by experiences that cannot immediately be interpreted by familiar words or symbols. Some may have difficulty speaking about the intimate experiences of spirit and heart because they lack the words, while others may use excessive wordiness as a way of avoiding the personal impact of such experiences.

Finally, the death of certain images of God may trigger feelings remininscent of earlier childhood losses. I am aware, for example, that I clung to a paternalistic image of God for years after my own father died. I was nine at the time he passed away, and clinging to my old image of God provided me with some sense of ongoing relatedness to my father. When that paternalistic image of God finally died many years later, I re-experienced many of the feelings I had had concerning my father's death. Some of these were stronger with the passing of the God-image than they had been with my father's passing. In fact, my preconditioning to relate to God-as-father had helped me freeze my orientation to God. By holding this orientation so strongly, I was refusing to let my father die, and at the same time I was refusing to allow myself to grow in relationship with God.

While early childhood experiences and preconditionings of mind-set go deeper and are more germane to spiritual direction than most early God- or self-image associations, they still represent a level of personal psychology that resides above or before the most fundamental spiritual encounters. At the deepest levels, we shall all be afraid of surrender and of giving ourselves to God. It is as if all the associations and symbols we attach to spiritual experience are simply preliminaries to the true struggle. They will always be encountered, they must usually be recognized, and occasionally they must be dealt with through intentional understanding and correction. But they remain very much in the outer mansions of the interior castle. The real confrontations lie deeper within.

5. Encounter: Human Responses to Deeper Spiritual Challenges

In Chapter 3 I described two general categories of spiritual experience: unitive experiences, in which self-definition is suspended, and those that preserve self-definition. Both kinds of experience may present certain threats against which self-image may react and defend.

Either sensory or extrasensory experiences (both of which preserve self-definition) may reveal insights about ourselves that we would much prefer to avoid. They may illuminate levels of our sinfulness that are too uncomfortable to accept, or cause recollection of past inadequacies and errors that may be too humbling. Similarly, such experiences may be accompanied by demands for some kind of self-sacrificing action. We might encounter old wounds and resentments that we are unwilling to forgive. Or it may become obvious that we must make peace with certain enemies, right some past wrong, or refrain from some pleasurable but destructive behavior. Some habits may need to be broken, some sources of gratification denied. Perhaps some service will need to be performed that will require more than we are willing to give.

If such insights and demands were seen as clearly and directly coming from God, if God were to speak out to us and say "Go and make peace with that enemy," or "Give a hundred dollars to this charity," we might not like it but we would probably hear the message clearly and respond to it in a forthright manner. But most spiritual experiences are not so direct and immediate. Most are far more subtle, open to a variety of interpretations, and therefore very susceptible to our stalls, distortions, or outright denials. We may forget (repress) an experience entirely, misinterpret it to our own advantage, or even spend all our energy in trying to figure it out rather than responding to it. Here, as in all areas of spiritual growth, we are constantly reminded of our own freedom and fear in hearing, seeing, and responding to that which the Lord presents to us.

Unitive experiences may pose any of these threats of insight and demand, but in addition they always represent the threat of dying-to-self. This is the fundamental threat of spiritual growth. In the suspension of self-definition that accompanies an experience of union, one does indeed die in a way and for a time. But this dying is usually not recognized in immediate awareness. On the surface, awareness is bright and clear, and at peace. There is usually no fear here, just open, simple, panoramic *being*. If one were able to comment about this level of the experience, all that could be said is that it is beautiful, complete, and absolutely true.

Simultaneously, at a "mid-level" of awareness, there is a bare recognition of dying. Without words or reaction, there is a noticing that self-determination and self-defining activity is ceasing, and that an entirely different way of being is happening. Here again, if comment could be made, the feeling would be seen as peaceful, liberating, superbly reconciling. It might be said that this is the positive, freeing side of death. But of course no comment can be made at any conscious level; to do so would re-assert self-definition and terminate the experience.

At a still deeper level, well beneath that of which one can be aware, some commentary does go on. There is an unconscious part of us that does not like dying in any way, at any time, under any circumstances. Regardless of how blissful and fulfilling the experience may seem to be in awareness, there is a part of ourselves that sooner or later will begin to complain. It is as if at some point beyond our awareness we cannot help but say "This has gone far enough; this has endured long enough. Much more of this and I will truly cease to exist. It is time to get back in the driver's seat again or I will be irrevocably lost."

As this unconscious reaction becomes louder and more emphatic, it finally breaks through into awareness and the experience fades. It may emerge in its direct form as fear of death, or it may be slightly refined into fears about losing control or being left alone in some spacious spiritual void. It may even be disguised as a commentary on how wondrous and beautiful it all is, and "Wouldn't it be nice to be able to hold on to this. . . ." Such attempts or desires to hold on to unitive realization are in fact simply methods of getting oneself back in control of things, and of course they invariably destroy the experience by re-establishing self-definition.

I have presented this threat as a fear of dying, but it could as accurately be seen as a fear of fully living. The implications and demands of even a brief unitive experience are awesome in terms of the full meaning of life. They destroy our false senses of mastery and autonomy; they present us with incontrovertible evidence of our connectedness to and utter dependence upon God and each other; they demand that love be freed into every moment and movement of our being. Dying or living, the implications are the same, and there is always a part of ourselves that rebels.

Defenses and Resistances

The human mind is an endless source of inventiveness when it comes to avoiding the implications of spiritual experience. Much of this avoidance can be seen in terms of the classic Freudian defense mechanisms about which so much psychology has been written.[1] According to this view, the mind responds to spiritual threats in much the same way it does to sexual or aggressive threats.

The first line of defense is repression. Here certain aspects of a spiritual experience or insight will be "forgotten," pushed beyond a preconscious level of awareness into an enforced unconsciousness. Often the entire experience will be repressed. This is especially true for unitive experiences, as exemplified by the fact that most people can remember only one or two major unitive experiences in their lives. But when a concerted attempt is made to recall such experiences, one can remember increasing numbers of them, even to the point of identifying that they occur—albeit briefly—numerous times each day. With sensory or extra-sensory experiences it is common that the most dramatic, exciting, and self-perpetuating aspects of the experience will be remembered, and those that pose the deepest threats will be repressed. Sitting in meditation, one may experience a variety of insights that seem significant and meaningful at the time, only to realize afterwards that nearly all of them have been "forgotten." This dynamic is exactly the same as that which occurs in the repression of dream memories.

If repression alone does not suffice, other defense mechanisms will be employed. The most primitive of these are denial and projection. In the former, one convinces oneself that a specific insight, demand, perception, or experience simply does not exist. In the latter, the thing is denied within oneself but seen disparagingly as occurring in someone else. Thus someone might say, "I have never felt any longing for God nor any desire to surrender. That's what those religious fanatics do. . . . They are always whining and mewling about God, God, God, and they cop out on their responsibilities in the name of religion. They all ought to be put out of their misery."

Sometimes this denial and projection can be focused on the spiritual director. For example, one directee said, "I think you must feel that I am not really worthy of God's love. I'm sure you're disappointed in me, sitting there and listening to me constantly struggling with the same old difficulties. But I know God loves me." The director in this instance quite naturally responded with a bit of defensiveness of her own: "What have I done or said to communicate that to you?" Struggling to find an example and unable to do so, the directee shortly came to recognize that it was his own feeling of unworthiness that he was experiencing, and it had simply surfaced as his opinion of what the director must be feeling. This enabled the discussion to move from the director-directee relationship to the relationship between the directee and God. This was more threatening, but also more to the point.

More "sophisticated" defense mechanisms such as rationalization or intellectualization are especially common among the theologically or psychologically educated. In rationalization one uses well thought-out justifications for devaluing or misinterpreting threatening insights and experiences.

I sometimes get a feeling in prayer that I am very childlike to God. I feel an urge to just whimper or say "Please God take care of me" like a baby. But of course that's just my own dependency needs and lack of trust in myself. I know that God has given me this mind and my whole adult being in order for me to use it to the fullest. It's only in actualizing myself to the fullest that I can express God to the fullest.

This man could not even for a moment accept the threat to his self-image posed by his natural and probably wholly legitimate aching to become as a little child in the face of God.

Intellectualization often takes the form of talking about spirituality as a way of avoiding spiritual experience. Thus, one may spend hours in spiritual direction or other settings seeking to refine one's understanding and comprehension of that which is fundamentally incomprehensible. All the while, it is possible to remain convinced that one is seriously searching, but this kind of search avoids the heart by limiting itself to the mind. This defense is especially difficult to deal with in spiritual direction as it can easily seduce the director into joining the discourse, especially if the topic is intriguing enough. It is in this way that some spiritual direction deteriorates into "spiritual conversation."

A closely related defense mechanism is isolation. Here, the emotional and heartfelt impact of a spiritual experience or longing is repressed, leaving only its cognitive or conceptual elements in awareness. "Yesterday in prayer I received the insight that God loves all of us unconditionally regardless of who we are or what we do. I knew this before, but it came to me much more clearly yesterday than ever before." In this situation the director was totally unable to get the directee to recount any feelings about the insight. Each time a feeling was asked for, more thoughts and conclusions were given.

"How were you feeling during this experience?"

"I felt that it made a lot of sense. Many things came together for me. I could understand some of the scriptures better."

In fact, the experience was accompanied by a sense of deep poignancy and sweetness that had nearly moved the directee to tears. But this was just too childish, too vulnerable, too threatening to be acknowledged. So it was "forgotten" and only the cognitive conclusions were remembered.

Displacement may well be the most common spiritual defense of our times. Here we seek to assuage our spiritual hunger through some physical, mental, or interpersonal activity that is not as threatening. Thus, we might seek to fill the void in our hearts by drinking, overeating, or taking drugs. Or we may seek meaning through hard work, intense relationships, or powerful conquests rather than through the more self-abandoning paths of spiritual growth. The displacement of spiritual passion and love for God into erotic encounters with other people is a classic experience that has been described by a number of spiritual searchers and has something to do with the establishment of celibate traditions.

Numerous other examples and defense mechanisms could be discussed, but it is more important for spiritual directors to know that such defenses can take place than to be able to label them precisely according to any specific system. It should be noted however, that all such defense mechanisms serve to preserve, protect, and promulgate one's self-image and self-importance in the face of spiritual truth. It should also be understood that the direct interpretation of such defenses is generally of as little help in spiritual direction as it is in psychotherapy. To say "I think you're just rationalizing there" may work if the defense is superficial and mild, but in cases where it really counts, such comments are more likely to produce increased defensiveness and denial than to enable any understanding.

It is better to try to determine what it is that is being threatened—why the person needs to be defensive—and then attempt to reassure and support the person in that area. For example, the man who was afraid of being childlike might be helped by some examples of other people who had similar struggles or by some acknowledgment that it might be possible to be both childlike and mature. As in psychotherapy, there is a proper time for this kind of support or for the direct interpretation of defenses. The discernment of this time is an art that both directors and therapists develop intuitively. But even more importantly, the spiritual director should not use personal knowledge or intuitive ability to analyze and objectify the directee, even if it is felt to be for the directee's own good. The business of spiritual direction, as I have asserted before, is that of attempting to remain attentive to God-in-the-moment and remaining as open to the Spirit and as surrendered to grace as one can be. Then all these understandings and analyses fall into their proper place. They are not to be used as spiritual instruments, but simply as ways of sharpening the edge of that true instrument of spiritual direction which is the surrendered spiritual director.

Resistances to Spiritual Practice

Psychological defenses may also impinge dramatically upon prayer life or ascetical practice. For example, resistances to prayer may be the result of wanting to avoid some psychological feeling or experience that threatens to surface if one becomes quiet and relaxed. Many people have been mystified to find that when they are the most troubled and stressed, when it seems they are most in need of quiet prayer and reflection, they are in fact the least likely to take the time for it. At such times it seems we are always coming up with some excuse for not praying, there isn't time, there are too many other pressing obligations, or we just forget. Even when we do pray, we are likely to avoid focusing on the areas of our lives that are most troubling to us. Sometimes we may fear a "failure" of prayer, a disappointment that would seem like God's rejection or disapproval. But in many cases these resistances really come from an underlying fear that the quiet openness of prayer is likely to confront us with something we are busily trying to avoid. The threatening issue may or may not be of a spiritual nature. More often than not it is simply some repressed psychological material that is threatening to surface.

We may also "forget" to pray about certain very troubling matters because we unconsciously fear that the prayer might work and we might be relieved of them. It is the hallmark of our neuroses, of course, that we cling to them while they make us suffer. To offer them to God or to truly seek their healing through prayer would confront us with the possibility of doing without them, and—unconsciously at least—this may be a decidedly unpleasant prospect. Regardless of the surface agony they produce, we maintain neuroses because they represent an unconscious "solution" to deeper psychological threats. Neurotic symptoms allow the energy of certain feelings or impulses to be expressed without their true nature entering awareness. Until these underlying factors are brought into awareness, we have no real choice about the matter. In addition, we resist change in our neurotic patterns simply because we "would rather bear the ills we have than fly to others that we know not of."

There are many other sources of psychological resistance to

spiritual practice. Some of us rebel against discipline and authority and thereby have great trouble setting and adhering to a scheduled time for prayer. In such cases, we are rebelling against our own internal "parent" who tells us we should or should not do something. Or we may seek "highs" of experience in prayer; we may have expectations for pleasurable sensations or relief from distress and become covertly angry or depressed when these expectations are not met. This may lead to resisting further prayer either out of an angry "I'm not going to do it if there's nothing in it for me" or out of a more depressive "I just don't think I can handle being disappointed again."

On the other hand, one may work even harder at prayer if expectations are not met. This is more characteristic of those among us who cannot stand the idea of being a quitter and who refuse to take no for an answer. But working harder at prayer is almost certain to backfire, for it carries the assumption that the quality or effectiveness of prayer is a function of one's own effort rather than a graced gift. The phenomenon of taking on increasing responsibility and effort in prayer during periods of frustration is very common, and most spiritual directors can recall having done this in their own experience.

Ironically, one may have great trouble praying after going through an especially beautiful, consoling experience. Such experiences often imply considerable unconscious threat to self-importance in spite of their overt beauty. One's reaction to this may sometimes be to turn away from prayer for a while, and one may be mystified as to the reason. If the deeper levels of self-image could talk, they might explain this behavior by saying "Yes, the experience was beautiful indeed. And it was most certainly what you long for, a deeper, more profound realization of your being in relationship to God. BUT, it's just a bit too much. It makes us afraid. We'd be better off going more gradually. No sense rushing into anything. Let's just back off for a while and pick up again when we've got a stronger sense of self-control."

Nearly everyone has had the experience of being unable to find "quiet" in prayer. We may overcome our initial resistances to prayer discipline only to find our minds filled with agitated, distracting clutter. With patience, perseverance, and vigilant wakefulness much of this clutter will settle down and more times of spacious openness will be given. Yet there are times when the noise seems to continue unabated over extended periods of time. Careful discernment and guidance is essential here, for such situations can occur for a variety of reasons. Perhaps the noisiness is a psychological defense against experiencing some threatening idea, impulse, or feeling. Perhaps it is a rebellion against self-imposed discipline. Perhaps it is a direct defense against becoming quiet, for in quiet one is not doing anything, and not-doing is sometimes frighteningly close to not-being. Or it could be that some more external force or spirit is actively attempting to subvert prayer. Finally, it could be that one is legitimately being called to some other form or style of prayer or that the Lord is actively depriving the soul of certain expected gratifications.

Careful examination needs to be made of such issues as the precise nature of the difficulty (what actually constitutes the distraction and how does it do its distracting); how it arises and disappears; subtle senses of good or evil in the experience; its effects upon one's faith and confidence in God; the presence or absence of threatening symbols or images in prayer, fantasies, or dreams; its apparent effects upon compassionate action, selfishness, and the essential spiritual freedom of the individual; and whether the person is praying for relief from the problem. This latter point is especially helpful to consider, as it reveals the stance of the individual's will in the matter. Psychological resistance is often accompanied by "forgetting" to pray for help and mercy; more precisely spiritual difficulties are often associated with humble, surrendering, seeking prayers that both ask for help and express an acceptance of "Thy will be done."

Another defense against spiritual practice, perhaps just as common, and in a sense, even more destructive, is the establishment of a pattern of prayer that is repeated diligently but includes no real willing openness to the Spirit. Here one finds a way of "going through the motions" of prayer, perhaps even to the point of spending long periods of time in silence, but while everything looks good on the outside, one's inner awareness is dulled, restricted, and closed off. Often this takes the form of a frozen, semihypnotic trance that allows the person (and sometimes the director) to believe that prayer practice is "perfect." Yet nothing seems to be happening at a soul-level. In describing this, I am reminded of similar adjustments that people sometimes make to psychotherapy. On occasion, a person will learn how to "play" at psychotherapy, talking about seemingly important issues, feeling apparently important feelings, seeming to ingest helpful insights, but all the while avoiding being touched and evading any impact that might lead to real change. People can sometimes learn how to "play" at prayer in much the same way, convincing both themselves and their directors that all is going well. The only real guideline here is the determination of whether there is anything happening in the person's overall spiritual growth. In the absence of struggle, one must at least question the reality of growth. Such distortions of prayer practice are much more difficult to deal with than prayer that is riddled with distractions, because there is complacency in the former and distress in the latter. However unpleasant the distress may be, it at least indicates that energy is active and dynamic. In complacency, energy is frozen.

Psychodynamic Changes in Spiritual Growth

Our psychological minds do not simply respond to specific emotional or spiritual experiences or disciplines, they also respond to the ongoing course of spiritual maturation. In other words, we react to the changes that the Spirit causes in us. Early in the process of spiritual growth, for example, a person may experience a time of special feelings of self-affirmation in faith. This may occur both as a result of experiencing God's love more intimately and as a consequence of learning the gentleness of mind and willingness to confront oneself that are necessary in prolonged quiet prayer. Thus in spite of whatever underlying threats to self-image there may be, the person may consciously feel transiently much more self-assured and comfortable. If prior to this he or she had relied extensively upon the supportive responses of other people for self-affirmation, the emergence of this newfound assurance might cause a significant change in behavior with others. While it could be hoped—and expected—that this would eventually lead to greater sensitivity and compassion for others, it is possible that the individual may transiently appear to friends and family as less open, less caring, less needing of them. They may feel shut out of the person's emotional world because in reality the person does not need them in the same way as before. All of this can happen unbeknownst to the individual, who may be very surprised when a loved one finally asks "What has come over you lately?"

While this fresh freedom is usually short-lived (it is generally replaced by deeper and more subtle levels of spiritual self-doubt later) it can be significantly disturbing for all concerned. Family members may relate the change to an individual's prayer or spiritual direction and accuse the person of escaping into a false spiritual world.

The process of spiritual searching may give rise to a wide variety of other emotional responses that can affect a person's social relationships. Sometimes a great amount of anger surfaces, related to reprocessing of old religious baggage or to frustrated attempts at achieving some special experience in prayer. This anger may be carelessly vented against family members, further increasing their suspicion as to the validity of the person's spirituality. At other times sexual feelings may grow into prominence, partly from displacement of deepening passion for God, and partly from purely liberated creative energy. This can be either disturbing or pleasing to others, depending on the context and manner in which this energy is expressed.

Appreciations of the power of prayer and the awesomeness of grace may stimulate surges of apparently evangelistic fervor that can also go overboard when indiscriminately expressed to others. While the individual may simply be trying to celebrate and share some newfound joy, others may feel an attempt is being made to convert them or that a challenge is being lodged against their faith or their way of life.

As we have mentioned, ascetical practice and spiritual growth may be associated with the appearance of enhanced intuitive or extrasensory abilities. A person may develop rapidly in the capacity to perceive and understand others at deeper and deeper levels, and if such insights are expressed carelessly or tactlessly, considerable anxiety or anger may be provoked.

While many of these untoward reactions from other people could be prevented by careful discretion on the individual's part, it is often not until after some negative encounters that the individual even begins to realize that discretion is needed. As a result of these reactions, the person is likely to receive many mixed messages about his or her spiritual searching. Some people will affirm and support it while others will be "turned off" and deeply threatened. Concern and negativity in one's environment greatly compounds one's own insecurities in the course of spiritual growth, and in most environments there will be very little real support or understanding. The careful appraisal of this environmental interaction is one of the more important and least remembered dimensions of spiritual direction. The director does not see the directee clearly if the vision is only of the directee's private journey with God or of the directee as part of an identified group of spiritual pilgrims. The directee has other relationships, very important ones, that are bound to be affected and that must be taken into consideration.

One executive decided to begin an intentional daily prayer practice, and to enter spiritual direction, after a profound spiritual experience that had occurred on a hunting trip. He told his wife about the experience and his decisions, and while not really understanding it, she responded supportively. But after a few weeks, the man noticed that every time he would retire to his den to pray, his wife would create some distraction. She would turn the television volume up or yell at the children or slam doors. He became very angry about this, and after asking her several times to keep things quiet, he finally exploded. "It seems like it's not asking too much for you to give me fifteen minutes of quiet once or twice a day. What's the matter with you anyway?" At this, his wife burst into tears and vented her own angry feelings. She felt his withdrawals for prayer were attempts to get away from her. She felt abandoned and bereft during those times but had been unable to express this before because as he had said, fifteen minutes once or twice a day did not really seem like too much. In processing this with his wife and later with his spiritual director, the man realized that in part his prayer time had been designed to get away from his wife. He had chosen times that previously had been periods of working together, getting the children ready for school in the mornings and off to bed in the evenings. These times had seemed "convenient" for the man, but in fact had been real abandonments for his wife. In other circumstances, his wife would have expressed her dissatisfaction more quickly and directly, but she was already quite ambivalent and fearful about what her husband's newfound spirituality might do to their relationship and, as she put it, "It's hard to criticize someone's prayer. I mean it wasn't like he was running around with some other woman or anything; he was *praying*. How do you get angry with somebody *praying?*"

The surface problem was solved here when the couple was able to agree on a more realistic time for the husband to pray. And after a while, the wife was more deeply reassured as she saw that her husband was not going to "turn into a religious fanatic or run off to a monastery or decide that celibacy would be a good idea." Even with the passage of time, however, the private spiritual journey of one spouse can continue to be subtly threatening to the other. It involves levels of personal experience that cannot fully be shared, and in marriages that are not used to affirming the spouses' individualities this can be continually disconcerting.

In attending to the larger sphere of the directee's interactions with and effects upon others, the director needs to ask questions such as How has your behavior changed as a result of what is happening in your spiritual life? Have other people noticed any differences in you? What have been their reactions? How do they feel about your practice? How much of your experience do you share? How well do you feel they understand you? And how well do you think you understand them? A balance must be kept between indiscriminate sharing and expression of one's spiritual experiences on the one hand, and excessive privatistic secretiveness on the other. More often than not it falls to the director to help provide this perspective.

It is well known that spiritual growth is accompanied by a gradual lessening of attachment to various desires. In the beginning, one may quite accurately perceive that nearly all one's motivations come from some form of attachment, from the desire to gain pleasure and avoid pain, to ensure security and success, and to avoid loss of control. But in the course of spiritual maturation, these sources of motivation begin to wane—often without the individual immediately realizing it—and this can cause some real consternation.

Often the first sign of this difficulty is the appearance of a mild, low-level sadness, which begins to color a person's overall attitude. This does not usually reach such a degree as to be called depression, for the individual usually continues to function well and tends to maintain a positive vision of the future. But laughter may not come quite so easily, and pensiveness or quiet self-reflection and feelings of uncertainty may happen more frequently. It is my impression that this is usually the result of a subtle, underlying grief process. At some level, one becomes aware that certain things that used to be vitally important (such as financial success, praise, accomplishment, or interpersonal popularity) are no longer quite so meaningful. Even some hobbies and recreational activities may go by the wayside. Often one does not spend quite as much time reading books or seeking other entertainments as before. This is not to say that such activities and investments actually disappear; they just become less important and less demanding of time and energy.

All of this represents a loss—not a loss of the things themselves, but of one's investment in them. Even so, it is a very real loss, and at some level, what is lost will be mourned. This mourning is likely to happen regardless of whatever new freedom or liberated loving may replace these old attachments. Again, these are often short-lived phases, because attachments keep recurring and revising themselves as the journey continues. In addition, certain underlying previously unconscious attachments come to awareness as the more superficial ones are alleviated, and these deeper attachments are often so strong and so troublesome that there may be only a limited time to mourn the loss of the others.

Concurrently with this lessening of attachments, it is likely that people will go through periods of distress related to decreasing confidence in old assumptions they have held about self, life, and world. For example, one woman said that she was feeling uneasy and close to tears . . .

Because it seems I don't really know what I'm doing anymore. I used to have a nice solid sense of who I was and where I was heading in life. I used to be able to decide what I wanted for myself and plan for it, and go out and get it. Now, because it seems more important to wait for God's call and to give myself to God's purpose, I'm at a loss as to what to do with all my drive and ability to figure things out for myself. It seems now that so much of my knowledge is contrived and not really on target. I trust in God, but it's still frightening. And there's something sad about it, not to be able to rely so much on my own resources.

This sadness and uncertainty represent a movement towards the "not-knowing" that accompanies lessening of attachments. Normally this does not occur so rapidly that severe fear or depression develops, but the low-grade sadness and restlessness can easily grow if one is not helped to understand their origins. This is especially true in our modern culture that so consistently values self-determination and accomplishment and devalues not-knowing and humility. Simple discussion of the process of lessening attachments and its consequences can alleviate much of the heaviness of these reactions, and it can also serve to test whether something more significant or disruptive, such as a self-imposed quietism, might be going on. In most instances, the recognition of these reactions as responses to spiritual growth is sufficient to allow a concurrent realization that life is in fact proceeding as efficiently as ever; that one is functioning at least as well if not better than before; and that faith is stronger and interpersonal relationships more loving than ever.

There are, however, periods during which one may not function so well and in which efficiency may really be compromised. Sometimes such times have been identified as "divine madness," but regardless of labels, any significant aberrations in adjustment to spiritual growth need very careful attention and appraisal. For example, a person might respond to an apparently lessened attachment by going overboard in the opposite direction. One young man had been so obsessed with performing well at his job and behaving in an exemplary manner that he reacted to what appeared to be a lessening of this attachment by "goofing off" at work and easing a great many of his behavioral controls. He did not take what others said seriously, and he made light of his own and others' values. He nearly lost his job before he came to his senses.

What had happened here was not a real lessening of attachment, but an unconscious—and partially preconscious—realization that attachments *could* be lessened. He used this insight to force upon himself an artificial liberation from the responsibilities that had been weighing him down, and he convinced himself that his action was a legitimate spiritual development. In fact, it was nothing more than the defense of reaction formation, an expression of attachment to the opposite of that to which one is really attached. Such experiences are quite common in pop-psycho-spiritual circles where radical and rapid personality revamping is attempted without the benefit of careful follow-up and critical evaluation. Perhaps the most frequent example of this is the usually passive person who, fed up with being treated like a doormat, learns some assertiveness techniques and becomes obnoxious. The accountability and evaluation inherent in legitimate spiritual direction should prevent, or at least minimize, such aberrations, but only if their possibility is kept in mind.

The two most general and pervasive psychological maladjustments in spiritual growth are the spiritual "cop-out" and spiritual narcissism. Most of us are quite familiar with the cop-out, in which one uses spiritual insight or practice to avoid dealing with daily responsibilities. Here meditation may constitute an escape from the world rather than a way into it, prayer may be used as a tranquilizer, and what goes under the label of spiritual surrender may be nothing more than self-enforced, theologically rationalized passivity or submission to one's own or someone else's ego.

Spiritual narcissism consists of using spiritual insights or practice to increase self-importance rather than to deepen humility. Here one finds the "holier-than-thou" attitude or subtler feelings of pride or power. The intricacies of spiritual narcissism are so complex and subtle that no one can escape it entirely. Am I pleased, sometimes, about my humility? Do I think that maybe I have finally "learned how" to pray? Do I sense that I am "able" to surrender? Have I "overcome" some sinful tendency? Spiritual narcissism involves the taking over of spiritual growth phenomena and the substituting of personal pride for humble gratitude.

The misplaced and distorted surrenders associated with both spiritual "cop-outs" and spiritual narcissism fail to meet the criteria for legitimate spiritual surrender. These criteria require that the surrender: (a) be a conscious act, (b) be freely and intentionally chosen, (c) involve acceptance of responsibility for the act of surrendering and all its consequences, and (d) not be directed towards any delimitable fully known object.

Depressions, Desolations, and "Dark Nights"

Spiritual development is characterized by a plethora of experiences in which mind, spirit, and heart all play a role. There are, as we have seen, psychological reactions to spiritual experiences, spiritual experiences that are mistaken for primary psychological changes, psychological phenomena that masquerade as spiritual experiences, and a host of other combinations. Among all of these one may detect classic God-given consolations and desolations as described in historic spiritual literature.[2] Sometimes God is felt as deeply present, loving, guiding, sustaining. At other times one feels only the absence of God. And occasionally one encounters a state that seems devoid of all experience.

Such events are generally expected and accepted in spiritual direction. In psychotherapy many of these would tend to be seen as problems to be solved, but the legitimate spiritual director would not be interested in substituting consolation for desolation, bringing light into a "dark night," or "working through" feelings of God's absence, if such experiences are seen to be part of God's action in a person. A directee may need support, reassurance, and encouragement during such times, but often this is communicated sufficiently by the director's careful listening and understanding presence. Both parties may then share the perception that these are conditions to be *seen through* rather than *worked through*.

The critical consideration in all of this is the source of the experience. If a period of emptiness in prayer can be attributed to some psychological block or self-defeating behavior on the part of the directee, one should, of course, move to try to correct it. On the other hand, if it can be discerned that the emptiness is a natural and graced event in the course of spiritual growth, one does well simply to let it happen. In many cases this discernment is made by default. In other words, a person experiencing emptiness in prayer will spontaneously try to change methods, exert more discipline, and seek to overcome any blocks that can be identified. If this is not successful, he or she may then give up and allow matters to take their natural course. This is not a bad way of doing things in most cases, especially if spiritual direction is conducted carefully. But there can be problems.

If one tries very hard to "produce" spiritual experiences during a period of emptiness, (or at any other time for that matter) the result will almost certainly be frustration. If this approach is not radically shifted or if one does not permit oneself to give up at this time, the frustration may well become destructive. If one cannot give up, an experience of open anger towards God in such situations is probably the most healthy of resolutions to the frustration of trying too hard. It allows the energy of the frustration to surface in free and flexible ways. More often, however, this anger remains covert and expresses itself as resistance to continuing practice, as a rejection of previously held values in daily life, or as a willful alienation of oneself from God. This alienation is not the same as feeling anger towards God. I can be angry with you and still be loving you and seeking reconciliation. Or I can alienate myself from you and seek the destruction of our relationship. The one is full of creative possibilities, but the other is full of death.

If the energy of frustration in prayer is neither surrendered nor experienced as anger, it may be turned against oneself and breed a true depression. In this case, the person feels increasingly unworthy and inadequate. Social withdrawal and irritability may occur. Continued prayer is extremely difficult, not only because of the absence of consolation, but also because the quiet of prayer involves encountering one's own disparaged mind and heart.

When depression like this occurs in the course of spiritual practice, it needs direct attention. The first form this attention should take is an examination of all possible causes that can be identified. Often, tracing the origin and development of the depression will enable sufficient clarification of the problem. The spiritual director may probe gently for any feelings of anger that the directee is able to acknowledge. The more these can be brought out, the more energy will be freed for creative action. While many people have trouble identifying actual anger in such situations, they may be able to acknowledge milder forms of the same emotional energy. Thus it may be helpful to use less severe words in the exploration: I guess you must feel frustrated about all this. Do you sense a little annoyance? Can you identify a little feeling of aggravation now and then? Any resentment?

While the identification and expression of angry feelings may help liberate blocked energy in mild depressions, physical activity is often even more effective. A good regimen of scheduled physical exercise is helpful for prayer life at any time, but it is especially so when one is struggling with angry frustration, resistance, or tension. At one level, exercise permits the expression of emotional energy directly. Since there is no need for the specific emotions to come into awareness, the usual defenses against them are bypassed. At a deeper level, disciplined physical activity frees the basic energies of body and mind, creating a thawed-out and flexible orientation. For psychological reasons, it is usually important that this kind of exercise be done for its own sake. Physical labor required as part of one's employment or needed to meet some other demand is nowhere near as effective in liberating energy as the same amount of exercise done routinely for its own sake as part of a daily schedule.

The exercise should be strenuous enough that its effects can be felt. It should produce at least some perspiration, acceleration of pulse or muscle fatigue. Of course good physical condition is a prerequisite for such undertakings. If there is any doubt at any time, a medical examination should be encouraged. In addition, or if need be as a substitute, gentle stretching and breathing exercises such as those of hatha yoga will accomplish the same ends. These are even more effective as regular preparations for quiet prayer. As well as liberating energy, they also help to create a relaxed and alert state of mind, cutting through much of the mental noisiness that can interfere with prayer.

In all of this, however, it remains important to make as accurate a discernment as possible as to how much depression is really accompanying or causing experiences of emptiness in prayer. If one has to err in this, it is probably better to label a true spiritual desolation as depression than the reverse. If one is in fact sensing a true desolation or "dark night" experience, even if it is accompanied by some reactive depression, attempts to remedy the depression will meet with minimal success at best.[3] The process of the desolation will continue, and the attempt to identify and deal with depression, by its very failure, may help clarify the true nature of what is going on.

On the other hand, if one hastily and blithely labels depression as a spiritual desolation or "dark night" experience, the depression will not be addressed and the sufferer may become needlessly confused about the nature of true spiritual desolations. This error is quite common, and in some cases it can be a way of using one's spirituality to avoid confronting uncomfortable psychological material—a "spiritual cop-out." I was recently told by a friend that she was going through a "dark night of the soul" because she was in a turmoil about her job. She was struggling with vocational decisions, with what she felt called to do and what she actually wanted to do. She had become somewhat depressed about the whole business. This was clearly not a dark night of the soul in any classic sense and such a blithe description indicates deep misunderstanding—or perhaps unconscious misuse—of the term.

While there is room for some flexibility in the meaning of such terms as "desolation" or "dark night," and while the classic descriptions of these experiences may not be completely applicable to contemporary spirituality, one does need to have a clear sense of their nature.[4] This is especially important in distinguishing the "dark night" from psychological reactions, for whatever it is, the dark night is decidedly not the product of one's psychological adjustment to life or to God. While not claiming any ultimate authority here, I will share with you my way of making some of these distinctions.

In the natural course of spiritual growth, one goes through many ups and downs. Some of these seem primarily determined by the experiences of daily life: frustrations, successes, losses, and failures in work or relationships. Some may be related to deeper psychological issues, old psychic wounds and resentments that surface in response to introspection or to some symbolic trigger. Some are physiologically determined, resulting from changes in brain chemicals. All of these are primarily within the realm of one's psychology, but they will inevitably affect and be affected by one's prayer life and spiritual awareness. As we have seen, for example, depression may interfere with prayer, and experiences in prayer may contribute to or alleviate depression.

When one feels very "down" about prayer and the spiritual life, and if the prayer experience is the cause of this, and if it is seen as coming from God, I think it is appropriate to call this a desolation.

Here, the prayer experience colors one's overall attitude towards life rather than one's life-attitude coloring prayer experience. Similarly, if reassuring and rewarding prayer experiences are seen as coming from God and spreading optimism, lovingness, and cheer into daily life, these may be called consolations. For some, this differentiation between what comes from God and what comes from ourselves may seem like the very kind of compartmentalization I cautioned against in Chapter 3, but I feel it is very important in order to avoid confusion at these deeper levels. Consolations and desolations can come in ways other than through formal prayer, but they must be seen as of divine origin. This implies that the individual's perception of these phenomena, as clarified in spiritual direction, is of critical importance. If changes in experience are legitimately seen as God-given, and if this understanding is used in no way to avoid anything, then I feel the terms consolation and desolation can be applied. To reiterate, consolations and desolations can include one's psychological reactions and mood changes in response to experience that is seen as God-initiated.

"Dark night" experiences, I think, need to be seen somewhat differently. There are many authoritative descriptions of the dark night, and people tend to view it in different ways.[5] For me, it is most helpful to see such experiences as not being influenced by one's personal psychological responses. They are deeper and more profound than any of the "ups and downs" of the spiritual life, regardless of how dramatic or painful the latter may be. To be fully accurate, one should probably not call the dark night an "experience" at all. It is more a deep and ongoing process of unknowing that involves the loss of habitual experience. This includes, at different times and in different ways, loss of attachment to sensate gratification and to usual aspirations and motivations, loss of previously construed faith-understandings, and loss of God-images. Accompanying this, of course, are loss of self-image/importance and of preconceptions about one's own identity.

All of these losses go on gradually, as part of the continuing process of "unknowing," deepening humility and self-abandonment. In terms of the dark night, we can hardly even use the term "realization" in its normal way, for what is involved is more a subtraction of prior knowings than an addition of new insight. The dark night then, is not so much an experience or a phase of development but rather the essence of one's ongoing spiritual journey. However, one does notice or recognize this process more acutely at some times than at others, and these "noticings" constitute what we may call experiences of the dark night.

One may proceed a way along the spiritual path, experiencing a variety of more superficial ups and downs without being fully aware of the inner changes that are taking place. During this time, attention may be directed primarily to the experiences of prayer and the consolations and desolations that represent the surface waves of the journey. But underneath there is a deep and strong current in which one is likely to have been caught without noticing it. At some point an awareness of this underlying process begins to take place—without understanding and without bearings. Here one may begin to experience drifting in darkness, a recognition of not-knowing. It may well appear that there is no worthy guidance in this drifting, the current is too deep and subtle to be identified. One may feel quite literally at sea, and utterly dependent upon and abandoned to the unknown and unknowable essence of God at the helm.

While spiritual growth does indeed deepen one's realization of the power and love and goodness and majesty of God, it presents an increasing spaciousness in which the eternal mystery of God that lies beyond these knowable attributes resides. Any glimpse of this spacious darkness can be devastating, yet it is probably never seen in anything remotely resembling its fullness. At one moment it may seem to be associated with the loss of specific attachments and motivations and may seem to raise the possibility of going beyond all attachment and motivation. At another point it may become manifest as a complete loss of understanding. At still another time, it may arise as the loss of some element of faith. And at yet another, it may feel like the total loss of God. Each such "noticing" constitutes a recognition of only a small part of the overall process in which one has become inextricably involved. These may be small glimpses, and even quite distorted, yet each can be profoundly shaking to human sensibility. It is only through grace, I feel, that we are blessed with our blindness to the totality of this process and our ignorance as to its ultimate implications. Were it otherwise, I suspect none of us would have the courage to embark upon the journey in the first place.

While it should be clear that these experiences—these noticings—have no psychological causation, there is bound to be a psychological response. This response, which may include fear, grief, despair, and not a little depression, needs to be seen as our reaction to noticing the dark night and not as a part of the dark night itself. In general, I think it is possible to differentiate between responses to experiences of the dark night and symptoms of primary psychological depression. Both primary depression and reactions to dark night experiences may include such phenomena as feelings of hopelessness, helplessness, agitation, and emptiness. Both may involve impoverishment of thoughts, absence of motivation, and loss of self-confidence. But some of the differences that I have perceived in working with people include the following:

1. Dark night experiences are not usually associated with loss of effectiveness in life or work, as are primary depressions. Often, in fact, the individual is mystified at how well he or she is continuing to function. This is especially true in terms of the individual helping others on their spiritual journeys.
2. Surprisingly, sense of humor is usually retained after dark night experiences. This humor is not cynical or bitter as it might be in mild depression; it retains an almost sparkling quality.
3. Compassion for others is, if anything, enhanced after dark night experiences. There is little or none of the self-absorption seen in clinical depression.
4. In the dark night, one would not really have things otherwise. While there may be great superficial dissatisfaction and confusion, the most honest answer, the deepest response, is that in spite of everything there is an underlying sense of rightness about it all. This is in stark contrast to primary depression, in which one's deepest sense is of wrongness and, consciously at least, the desire for a radical, even miraculous, change is pervasive.
5. A person experiencing the dark night does not seem to be pleading for help as does a clinically depressed person. Explanations and evaluations may be sought, but seldom is there communication of anything like "get me out of this."
6. Very subtly, yet perhaps most importantly, one does not generally feel frustrated, resentful, or annoyed in the presence of a person undergo-

ing a dark night experience. While such feelings are common in working with depressed people because of their own internalized anger, one is much more likely to feel graced and consoled with someone experiencing the dark night.

Some caveats need to be mentioned about these differences. They are all psychological observations, and as such they are intended to supplement, rather than substitute for, traditional methods of discernment. Further, they are generalities and cannot be applied arbitrarily to any given person. For example, a dark night experience may be accompanied by a primary depression of some other cause; in such a case the above criteria would be worthless. In addition, God-given experiences such as glimpses of the dark night are never really reducible to such specifics. There are always exceptions and surprises. Also, I wish to underscore again that whenever spiritual directors use any kind of criteria for objective evaluation as a substitute for their own prayerful, surrendered openness of heart, they do an injustice to their directees. Objective evaluations have a place, but that place is always secondary.

Finally, consideration must be given to the possibility that certain experiences appearing to be consolation, desolation, or "noticings" of the dark night might in fact be the work of evil. It is not within the purview of this book to provide adequate guidelines for such discernments, but I will take this opportunity to suggest a few supplemental questions that I have found to be helpful: Is there a healthy openness about the experience; is the directee willing to have it examined from all perspectives? Does it feel honest, loving, and faith-enriching to you as the director regardless of how it feels to the directee? Does it seem to be helping, or crippling, the directee's reliance upon God? Is it nurturing or impeding the directee's love for God and neighbor? Finally—and I think most importantly—how is your immediate, prayerful awareness affected as you discuss the matter with the directee? Does it lead you into a deeper sense of God's presence and grace or does it lead you into coldness, alienation, antagonism, or selfishness?

When the question of evil arises in a discussion with a directee, I often pray silently while the directee speaks, sensing how this prayer comes to me. Encounters with God-given, graced experiences bring this prayer in me easily, deeply, and calmly. Encounters with evil seem to disrupt or even prevent it altogether. Again, these are supplementary suggestions and should not be used arbitrarily or in lieu of complete discernment.

If, as is often the case, after all the discriminations have been attempted there is still no definite sense as to whether one is dealing primarily with psychological or more precisely spiritual phenomena of good or evil nature, it is necessary to pray further and to wait longer, so that the fruits of the experience can be evaluated. Occasionally a psychiatric evaluation may be helpful if there is a significant disruption of a person's daily life or an intractable "stuckness" in the spiritual arena. But as we shall discuss in Chapter 8, this must be undertaken carefully. If such consultation is not deemed necessary, it is probably a good idea to keep looking for depression, for example, in every possible way as long as a "down" experience persists. It can be very reassuring to both director and directee to know that while significant psychological factors have not been found, every attempt has been made to identify them. The same thinking applies to considerations of possible evil-natured phenomena. Knowing that the negative, destructive possibilities are being considered can allow greater confidence in one's experience. This is far better than any hasty attempt to identify a "down"—or an "up," for that matter—as being of direct, God-initiated origin.

Most people in spiritual direction know enough about modern psychology to mistrust many of their spiritual experiences. This is a healthy wisdom if it is used to raise questions and avoid hasty conclusions, but it is not helpful if it is used to reduce all spiritual phenomena to the realm of psychology. It is important for spiritual directors to share their psychological knowledge and their healthy mistrust in a forthright and courageous way. Then, when a phenomenon is discerned to be of truly graced origin, the discernment will have value and the phenomenon can be fully appreciated.

6. Relationship: Interpersonal Dynamics in Spiritual Direction

Besides differing from psychotherapy in intent, content, and basic attitude, spiritiual direction is generally surrounded by a characteristic atmosphere that is seldom encountered in any other interpersonal relationship. This atmosphere is one of spaciousness and underlying peace; of openness and receptivity; of a kind of quiet clarity in which it is easier to allow and let be. As one person put it, "Being in spiritual direction is just like being in prayer, only there's someone with me in it."

For years I had been subtly aware of this difference in my own work. On certain days when I had scheduled some spiritual direction sessions in the midst of psychotherapy hours, I noticed an automatic relaxation and peacefulness that would settle over me when a directee came in. And after the session I would feel energized and rested, as if I had not been "working" at all. But the difference became even more clear during a conference in which I asked a group of hospital chaplains and pastoral counselors to pair up and briefly offer spiritual direction to one another. My instructions were for them to attend to the Holy Spirit in their interchanges, to be aware of seeking grace, and to recall as often as possible that the true healing, growing effects of spiritual direction come of God's work *through* the relationship rather than from their own purely autonomous efforts. Afterwards I asked them to compare this experience with their usual counseling situations. Typical responses were as follows:

I was relaxed here. It seemed as if I didn't really have to *achieve* anything. I could be more allowing and open than I ever am in counseling.

After a while it seemed as if it were all a kind of prayer. We were talking about all kinds of things, but I was in prayer . . . both of us were.

I felt refreshed and invigorated both during and after our talk. I let go of a lot of things, my own agendas and my efforts to steer things one way or another.

I felt a great difference in responsibility. Often I carry a heaviness about my clients, feeling I must be very careful to try to make things go right. I know counseling is a shared responsibility, but I can't keep from feeling its weight. Yet in this spiritual direction experience it was as if all that weight was lifted from me. I didn't shrug it off; it was really *lifted.*

It's difficult to express and it sounds paradoxical, but here where I'm dealing with what is obviously the most important part of a person's life, it's like my input is the *least* important. Maybe a better way to put it is that at this level I *can't* really know how things should come out. I still have to use all my faculties and my best judgments, but I am almost forced to surrender the ultimate outcome of things.

I was just being there, open, alert, and responsive, but just being. I was more intrigued by the power of God than by the specifics of my own abilities or by the drama of the other person's story.

I felt a real sense of participation. Not just being a part of the relationship, but of something immensely larger. It was humbling and at times a little scary, but it was also very peaceful.

It seemed to me that this is how *all* my counseling relationships should be. I've experienced the same kind of allowing and letting-be on rare occasions in counseling, but here it pervaded the entire session. I know that it couldn't have been anything *but* a healing experience for both of us.

These were men and women who viewed their usual daily work as ministry. Whenever they thought about it, they could state that in doing counseling they were expressing their faith, "coming from" their own senses of God's power and love in the world. They were able to proclaim that their counseling was "pastoral" because they were pastors and because they were God's representatives to the people with whom they worked. But as one of them said,

My being-in-God is something that I *know* to be true in my regular counseling work. It exists as a fact, behind all of my endeavors, and I can acknowledge it whenever I think about it or when someone asks me about it. Generally it just hangs around in the background, though, as a kind of underlying principle. But in spiritual direction it comes right up front. It is no longer just a background knowledge or inference, but a fully lived and experienced reality. I no longer know it in the usual sense. Instead, I *sense* it in its lively, loving action—in the immediate moment. It's like the difference between thinking about love and being in love, between knowing you are a swimmer and actually diving in and swimming.

Of course it would be idealistic to expect every moment of every spiritual direction situation to be filled with this immediate awareness of God. But I am certain one can expect many, if not most, moments to be so, and one can do everything possible to facilitate this awareness.

The Attention of the Spiritual Director

It is my belief that the primary task of spiritual directors is to encourage within themselves this moment-by-moment attention towards God as frequently as possible during spiritual direction sessions. It might be said that this is the primary task and desire of all spiritual seekers; it is also what the directee is looking for. But for the director to be of assistance to the directee in this, the director must first attend to his or her own realization. This underscores again the absolute necessity of personal attention to one's own prayer life and daily awareness of God, and of being in spiritual direction oneself.

During the course of any spiritual direction session, the director needs to keep remembering the reality of what is happening. A constantly repetitive reminding of oneself may be necessary here. It helps to begin the session with quiet prayer and with a silent plea for grace to help one truly be a channel of God's truth and love for the other person. During the session itself, it is usually necessary to keep re-orienting oneself towards God. There are times when this happens easily and naturally, and one can just "sail on through" with an almost constant immediate sense of presence in God. But there are many other times when it is not so easy. Personal concerns, private agendas, fears or desires for the directee or the relationship, or intriguing elements in the directee's situation may all serve to kidnap one's attention from this basic and immediate awareness. Often this kidnapping occurs simply out of habit. In most of our professional and personal relationships we are used to attaching our attention to the content of what is happening; we are concerned with the specifics of the interchange and with our own self-image. We become caught up in the words and feelings and problems and issues of the encounter.

This habit must be broken or at least suspended if spiritual direction is to be at its best. We must at least temporarily sacrifice not only our self-concerns but also our preoccupations with content and often even our personal interest in the directee. This latter element may be difficult to swallow at first, yet it may well be the most important factor for those of us who see ourselves as caring, loving facilitators of human spiritual growth. We are, paradoxically, the ones who are most likely to allow the importance of our personal caring to eclipse the divine love that may in part be expressed *through* our caring. Some practical accounts may help to make this more understandable.

Several spiritual directors were asked to monitor one of their direction sessions in terms of their own moment-by-moment awareness of the divine. They were asked to notice the specific times at which their attention was taken away from God and directed towards something "else." Some typical responses follow:

I guess I was most attentive to God during our silent prayer at the beginning. I have to admit that it seemed to go steadily downhill after that. She (the directee) was so caught up in trying to understand a prayer experience and so strongly looking to me for help with it that I gradually got caught up in it too. I guess I totally lost sight of God during the last half of the time. Not until the very end did I remember that I was supposed to encourage a prayerful attitude in myself.

I think I was inclining myself towards God most of the time. But there were two points where it was obvious that I got pulled away. The first was when he started talking about how helpful spiritual direction had been. I guess it threw me back into self-consciousness and got me thinking about how I hoped the direction would continue to be helpful. Then I sort of caught myself and took a couple of deep breaths and relaxed into a sense of graced presence between us. The second time was toward the end when I was sharing one of my own experiences with him. When I started talking, it seemed to flow naturally out of me—it seemed just right. But somewhere in the course of talking, I again became self-conscious. It had something to do with comparing his experience with mine.

One time stands out for me. It began when I suddenly started thinking about something I had to do later in the day. Then I realized I wasn't paying close enough attention to her so I brought my mind back to focus on what she was saying. Later still, I realized that I was being so careful to pay attention to *her* that I'd totally forgotten to be attentive to *God*. At that point I had to ask for us to have a few moments of silence so I could re-collect and recenter myself. From there on it went quite well.

I don't think there was a single instant during the whole time that I was really attentive to God or grace or the Spirit. He (the directee) came in so troubled about his marriage and he looked so depressed that all I could do was respond to his pain. I guess that's understandable, but what really troubles me is that not only did I not look for grace, I also failed to raise the possibility for him. I never even asked how his troubles had affected his prayer life or how he'd been praying about them, or how he saw God in what was going on. I was so caught up in trying to be understanding and helpful that I really don't think any spiritual direction took place at all. That's not to say it wasn't a good interaction. I think he felt better to know that I understood, and I certainly was being *pastoral*. I think he even got some helpful perspective on the situation. But I can't help wondering if it wouldn't have been more helpful and healing if I could have attended to the Lord in the midst of it all.

These examples give a hint of the wide range of naturally occurring things that can kidnap attention. It should be understood that there is nothing that is always or necessarily bad about such divergences. Many of them are to be expected as natural consequences of our incarnated humanity responding to itself and to others. But it should also be clear that such divergences can change spiritual direction into pastoral counseling, into therapy, into conversation, or even into manipulation without recognition on either person's part. When this goes on too far or too long, it becomes very easy for both parties to use the divergence unconsciously as a way of avoiding the spiritual reality of the moment.

We have discussed some of the intricate and subtle ways in which we unconsciously seek to avoid spiritual realization, some of the defenses and resistances that our personal self-importance throws up to circumvent surrender. Spiritual direction is by no means exempt from this, and if we do not maintain some degree of careful, open vigilance it is entirely likely that many spiritual direction relationships will come to involve no spiritual direction whatsoever. To reiterate, we need to be cognizant of the many kinds of factors that can pull us away from attention to God-in-the-moment, things such as personal cares and attachments; our sense of self-importance as spiritual directors; feelings of responsibility for how the direction goes; our hidden agendas and expectations; fears of our own spiritual surrender; attraction to the power of psychological understandings and psychodynamic explanations; personal attractions or repulsions about the person of the directee; and even our human concern for the directee's struggle.

It is neither possible nor desirable to rid ourselves entirely of such distractions. Many of them serve us quite well in other regards. Ironically, those that serve us most well—such as our human caring or our understanding of psychology—are the most likely to derail us in spiritual direction. But while we cannot and should not try to annihilate them, we can in every possible way keep reminding ourselves of what it is that we are truly about in spiritual direction. We can keep recalling and remembering where spiritual growth really comes from and where our eyes need to be focused. And we can keep resurrendering.

If it seems that this attention towards God constitutes a disregard for or inattentiveness to the directee, there are two perspectives that might be helpful to understand. The first involves an appraisal of different kinds of legitimate human relationships in terms of God, person, and attention:

In most *friendships or social interactions,* one might say, "Sometimes I lose myself in the pleasure of being with you. At other times I assert myself on the basis of my attraction or dislike for you. My attention shifts from myself to you, to our relationship, to myself again."

In most *business relationships* one could say, "I see you as a vehicle for helping me attain my objectives. Sometimes I may manipulate you, and at other times we may work as a team, but my attention is usually focused ahead of our interaction, on the goals of our enterprise."

In *teaching or parenting relationships* one might say, "I work hard to help you grow into what I think you need to be—even if that simply means your ability to be who you want to be. I give myself and my attention to the work of this, and I try to do it well for your benefit and my gratification."

In *medical therapy* one might say, "I sell you my time, attention, and expertise. You put yourself in my hands for a while, and I attend to what's best for you. I take this responsibility seriously, and while I do not enjoy the power I have over you, I must use it in doing my best to help you."

In *humanistic therapy* one could say, "I bring all that I am into this relationship with you. For the time we are together, I attend to you with all my heart and with all my expertise. I give my attention to our being together in the hope that this will facilitate your growth and health."

In *pastoral counseling* or other pastoral enterprises, it might be, "In the name of God I am here for you. I give my attention to you and to our being together as a representative of God's love and care for you. I am a broken, human expression of that love, but you have my attention and care while we are together and my prayers while we are apart."

In *spiritual direction,* one might say, "My prayers are for God's will to be done in you and for your constant deepening in God. During this time that we are together I give myself, my awareness and attention and hopes and heart *to God for you. I surrender myself to God for your sake.*"

In light of these statements, it may not seem quite so harsh or dualistic to say that concern for a person's feelings and experience can interfere with spiritual direction, or that focusing one's attention on the person might constitute being sidetracked from attention to God.

Even more helpful, though, is the second perspective, which has to do with the ideal quality of awareness during spiritual direction. In the discussion thus far it may have seemed that one must attend either to God or to the person. Such a dualistic interpretation is erroneous, and it stems from our usual habit of focusing attention. Throughout daily life most of our time is spent focusing attention first on this, then on that, then on something else. It is as if we wear blinders that allow us to perceive only that which is directly in front of us at any given time. Then we must turn our heads to attend to something "else." As long as we are locked into this way of seeing, we are also confined to a dualistic and compartmentalized reality. Here am I. There are you. Over there is God. This is me. That is a tree. This is our relationship. There is someone else.

In the quiet of contemplative prayer, it is sometimes possible to break out of these limits of perception. More accurately, perhaps, these limitations are broken *for* us. At such times we experience an opening of attention. The blinders around our eyes fall away, and we are granted a panoramic view that is inclusive rather than selective. As this vision expands, it is impossible to avoid sensing the reality of God. At the most open point, we no longer can even identify ourselves as the seers. Instead, it all becomes a oneness, a co-inherence that excludes nothing, yet is fascinated by nothing. Awareness is clear and awake to everything, yet focused on nothing special. There *is* nothing special here—or everything is equally special. The totality is all that exists, and one knows and feels immediately, without any need for inference or thought, that God is vitally and comprehensively present.

While it is not possible to achieve such awareness at will, it is one's willingness for and openness to this vision that is the best attention in spiritual direction. In my opinion, this is the way one can be attentive towards God in any situation. It does not ideally focus on God to the exclusion of oneself or the directee. Instead, one is careful to remain open and to ensure that attention to oneself or the directee or anything else does not eclipse this larger openness towards God. This is what it means to me to "be prayerful" in spiritual direction. From a practical standpoint, it involves assuming exactly the same mind-set and attitude in spiritual direction as one assumes in quiet prayer.

In the midst of this openness, as in prayer, concern for ourselves or the directee or something else will capture our attention from time to time. When this happens, it is as if we have put the blinders on again; we have reduced the field of vision and once again can see only that which is directly in front of our eyes. At such times God is either forgotten entirely or is reduced to a limited image that excludes our attention to anything else. Whenever this kind of restrictiveness of attention is noticed, as in prayer, it should be a signal to re-open ourselves as much as we possibly can. This involves a conscious, intentional act of relaxing and re-surrendering. We may not want to do this at the moment, because what is in front of our eyes may be very enticing and fascinating. It may be exciting and pleasurable, tragic and important, dramatic or poignant or fearful. We may desire to stay focused upon it "just long enough to take care of it." Or we may fear that by re-surrendering we will avoid the issue and not live up to our responsibility to it. It is very likely—and culturally expected of us—that we will use these kinds of excuses in most of our daily activities. But in spiritual direction our responsibility is most clearly to God in God's wholeness rather than to some self-selected and personally restricted aspect of that wholeness. I suspect that this is really true for all of life, but in spiritual direction, when care for another person's soul is at issue, it becomes of paramount importance.

In spiritual direction, if nowhere else, we must confront the unavoidable truth that "taking care of it"—whatever "it" may be— will happen of God and not of our singular personal willfulness. We may be instruments of God in taking care of something. We may be actual parts of Christ's body in God's work. But regardless of how intelligent or psycho-theologically sophisticated we may be, we eternally lack the ultimate wisdom to know how to take care of anything independently. Even if we cannot bring ourselves to admit this to ourselves in the rest of our life, we *must* accept it when it comes to the care of other souls. There is no psychological method, no theological treatise, no scriptural message, and no private or collective wisdom that can inform us of the full and ultimate desire God may have for a specific soul at a specific time. And even if we could somehow be privy to such divine knowledge, we would have no capacity to ensure a precise application of it. Accepting and affirming our human abilities for what they are, it is imperative in spiritual direction to recognize our utter dependence upon God.

This is, of course, humbling. And the way I have portrayed it may make it sound as if only saints could really offer spiritual direction. As normal mortal beings we do not remember our utter dependence upon God often enough, even when offering spiritual direction. Nor do we experience that degree of open clarity of attention often enough in spiritual direction or even in our own solitary prayer. And yet, as incomplete as we are in this, many of us are called to be spiritual guides for others. There is no doubt about this calling, and if those who are called avoid the task because of their humility and inadequacy, they will turn their backs upon an important part of their graced life in the world. It is grace, after all, that must enable us to respond.

Mother Teresa of Calcutta was once asked how she could continue to work in situations of irrevocable hunger and suffering. "God calls us to be faithful," she said, "not successful." In spiritual direction, one must keep remembering perfection, and one must take note as frequently as possible of the divergences and fixations of attention that occur, but it is neither realistic nor helpful to expect to be fully "successful." Whatever progress we may make towards perfection is granted and given to us through grace, just as is the progress of those who come to us for spiritual direction. Our role is to be willing for this to happen and to be remaining as attentive as possible to our own errors, refraining from them wherever we can. This is sufficient challenge.

It is for this reason that in speaking of the nature of awareness and attention in spiritual direction I have used words like "remember," "remind," "recall," and "re-orient" more often than "maintain," "hold," or "establish." I am convinced that even the best of the usual spiritual direction encounters are characterized by a shifting in and out of the director's attention towards God. Times of graced attentiveness towards the divine are punctuated by times of attachment and focused attention. Periods of open surrender are garnished with moments of willfulness. The director's human task in this is to notice what is happening as frequently and courageously as possible and to not indulge the divergences any more than necessary. There are perhaps a few saints among us who are not troubled by any such divergences, but I have never met one. I know a few people who seem almost constantly open and present to the Lord, and the spiritual power of these beings is truly awesome. But they too have their times of attachment, their "Achilles' heels of the ego."

The capacity to experience living moment by moment in God differs among us in matters of degree. Spiritual growth includes an enlargement of this capacity, but God calls people of varying degrees of capacity to be spiritual helpers for others. While we can do little on our own to advance in this regard, we certainly can recognize many of the areas and times in our experience when we are off the track. It is especially important to do this when offering spiritual direction. It is even more important not to label our divergences as being right. For this we need our own spiritual direction and our own willingness to subject our perceptions to the critique of scripture, tradition, and colleagues. Then, with grace, we may grow in spirit and as spiritual directors.

Spiritual Direction and Transference

While it is possible to remain attentive to many of the manifestations of grace in the direction relationship, it must also be assumed that grace functions in many ways of which we are unaware. In addition, we have seen that many personal and interpersonal unconscious forces exist that may work *against* the graced growth of the directee.

Recognizing this, it is necessary to understand the meaning of some classic psychological terms in relationship to spiritual direction. The first of these is *transference.* In popular usage, transference is taken to mean any feelings or behaviors that are unconsciously determined and are projected into a relationship with another person. It is further assumed that these feelings and behaviors constitute problems or difficulties within the relationship. Neither of these understandings is precisely accurate. In its true psychiatric meaning, transference refers to specific situations in psychotherapy in which a patient unconsciously invests the therapist with qualities and attributes pertaining to the patient's mother, father, or some other person of childhood significance and then proceeds to act as if the therapist really were that person.

This is to be distinguished from *parataxic distortion,* which is not limited to therapeutic relationships and simply consists of predetermined patterns of relating to people who have certain characteristics.[1] For example, I may relate differently at the outset to fat people and thin people, tall and short people, and men and women on the basis of my early childhood experiences with people of similar characteristics. This is parataxic distortion, a phenomenon all of us are subject to from time to time. It is a specific form of prejudice, an initial stereotyping of individuals on the basis of their external attributes and how these attributes trigger memories of early childhood interactions. If I experience transference, however, it must occur within the context of an ongoing relationship (usually psychotherapy or counseling) and consist of my actually "transferring" very specific feelings towards my father or mother upon the therapist. I may complain that she never understands me (though she clearly does), because of some feelings I have about my mother not understanding me. Or I may become very afraid of him because my father used to intimidate me. Then I might proceed to "act out" these feelings by wanting to terminate therapy or by seeking understanding or powerful intimacy in other relationships. Parataxic distortions become manifest at the beginning of relationships—at first meeting—and are often alleviated by getting to know the other person. On the other hand, transference develops gradually within a relationship and must be "worked through" to gain insight and perspective.

Parataxic distortions cause problems because they alter perceptions and can block potential relationships on the basis of reactions to "first impressions." In classic psychotherapy, however, transference is seen as fundamentally helpful. It is felt to be an essential component of psychoanalysis, an absolutely necessary prerequisite for a complete therapeutic process. According to Freudian thought, it is only with the development and subsequent resolution of a "transference neurosis" that therapy can be completed. It is for this reason that the analyst remains anonymous to the patient, sharing little of his or her personality. It is also why the analyst sits behind the patient, out of sight. These measures are intended to make the analyst a "blank screen" upon which the patient can project transferred attributes and feelings.

In face-to-face counseling, which is designed to deal with more superficial problems, transference is usually considered to be more trouble than it is worth, so it is actively avoided by the counselor's acting more like a "real person" in the sessions. Thus counselors may share a good deal of their personal experiences, reactions, and opinions. They may give advice and even conduct social or business relationships with their clients outside the counseling hour. Such behaviors minimize the likelihood of transference development.

Still, transference can occur in counseling and other similar settings. If the person's need and readiness to surface old conflicts are sufficiently strong, transference may happen even if great pains are taken to avoid it. This can lead to extremely complicated and "sticky" problems in relationships that are not geared to handle them. The most popularized of these complications are sexual liaisons that happen between counselors and clients for reasons that seem real enough to the parties involved, but are obviously trumped-up and contrived when seen by an outside observer. True transference is never completely one-sided. It may be initiated by the unconscious needs of a patient, or client (or directee), but once it fully develops, the helping person is inevitably also involved and responding at unconscious levels.

In terms of spiritual direction situations, it would generally be expected that transference, at least in its classic sense, would not develop to any great degree. If there is adequate understanding on the part of both director and directee that attention is to be given more to the divine than to each other, and if the director is sufficiently transparent in his or her own attentiveness, the likelihood of significant transference is dramatically reduced. Further, the relative infrequency of spiritual direction meetings (typically once a month) decreases the emotional importance of the director to the directee as compared to that in the far more frequent sessions of insight-oriented therapy. While very mild and inconsequential transference manifestations may arise in any ongoing relationship, transference should present real problems in spiritual direction only rarely.

But it can happen. Spiritual directors are often seen as authority figures and cast into parental roles by directees. While this usually remains within the realm of parataxic distortion, it can in some cases set the stage for transference. The mutuality of spiritual "friendships" is no insurance against this, especially if one party is seen as more spiritually "advanced." If the directee assumes a subservient or submissive position relative to the director, some parentally determined feelings are bound to arise. These do not as yet constitute true transference and can often be dealt with openly or counteracted by the director's sharing of his or her "real person."

But if significant transference does arise in spiritual direction it almost invariably causes a problem, because the director becomes a distraction, a source of preoccupation for the directee. Although, in its early phases this may simply involve admiring the director as a channel of grace, it is very likely to progress to admiring the director more than the grace. It is primarily the role of the director to see that things do not go this far, for the processes involved are occurring unconsciously in the directee. Transference, in whatever form it may take, should be recognized and dealt with as quickly as possible.

One of the most helpful ways of recognizing transference is to notice feelings of *countertransference*. In psychotherapy it has long been understood that one of the early signs of a developing transference is the emergence of certain feelings within the therapist. These may take the form of confusion as to what is actually happening in the sessions; a strong need to make things go right; talking more in the sessions; dreaming about the patient; or excessive worries, attractions, repulsions, hostility, or sympathy in relation to the patient. Sometimes there may simply be an uneasy feeling, a low-grade anxiety in connection with the sessions. Such manifestations can be indicative of the therapist unconsciously responding to the patient's transference, or they may mean that the therapist is transferring some of his or her own unconscious feelings to the patient. In either case, these signs should warrant a careful evaluation of the relationship.

These signals are perfectly applicable to spiritual direction. Here however, one must also look for changes in how the director prays for the directee, in the director's moment-by-moment awareness during the sessions, in the overall transparency of the interchanges, and so on. Whenever a directee seems to be taking on increasing importance or specialness in the mind of the director, this should be a signal to take a look at the relationship. It may be that the directee is simply going through an especially stressful or joyful time and the director is naturally responding to this as any other person would. An increasing sense of importance might also be a legitimate spiritual calling, indicating that something special needs attention or prayer. Or it could be transference. In any case, a close examination is required. As well as going through this examination privately, the director would do well to take it up openly with the directee, asking if he or she has sensed any change in the atmosphere of direction, and how he or she is feeling about the relationship in general. Such questioning is not likely to produce immediate clarification if a real transference is underway, but it will certainly provide important data and set the stage for further honest processing should the need arise.

Even if the director is unaware of changes in his or her own experience, transference issues can sometimes be identified on the basis of the directee's behavior alone. The directee may begin saying things that simply do not make sense, referring to the director in unrealistic ways, or misinterpreting the director's words and actions. Perhaps the directee will confide that images of the director have appeared in prayer or dreams. Or the directee may be pushing for a change in the relationship that does not seem constructive. Again, none of these phenomena automatically indicates transference. There could always be other causes of a psychological or spiritual nature. These examples are given for the purpose of raising questions about the possible existence of transference rather than as means of "diagnosing" it.

In the case of true transference in spiritual direction, it is likely that attempts to process it with the directee will initially prove confusing to both parties. Here it is especially important to encourage prayerful attentiveness on the part of both, to refrain from any significant changes in the relationship, and to be especially cognizant of alterations in awareness and attention. If the director and directee can be honest and courageous enough to stay with the process, clarity will come in time. On rare occasions, some consultation may be needed if the direction relationship becomes confounded and feels truly "stuck." This can take several forms, including processing it with one's own director, presenting the situation to colleagues or a supervisor, or calling up a sympathetic psychiatrist or psychologist. As we shall discuss in Chapter 8, one must be cautious about preserving anonymity and confidentiality in such undertakings.

Once transference is solidly identified, it will be necessary to see if its process can be stopped. Sometimes it is possible to accomplish this with simple recognition of the source and manifestations of the transference. Occasionally some time can be given to trying to "work it through." But if the transference is strong and persistent, it is usually better that the directee find another director. In the midst of significant ongoing transference, gross misperceptions and strong attachments are unavoidable, and spiritual direction can be seriously compromised. The simple occurrence of transference is not an indication for either termination of the relationship or referral for psychotherapy. But sometimes the complications and distress caused by the transference will themselves warrant one or both.

It is especially important here not to jump to any quick conclusions, but to keep looking for the graced potential in what is happening. Just because transference creates problems in spiritual direction does not mean that it cannot be a graced event. Just as God works through our personal unconscious craziness, God can also work through distortions in relationships.

Other Complications

Transference and parataxic distortion are primary psychological phenomena. That is, they are responses to psychological factors in one's personal history. In spiritual direction one also encounters phenomena that are psychological responses to spiritual factors. These too usually take place at an unconscious level and can often involve both director and directee.

Nearly all spiritual direction relationships experience a growth in intimacy as time progresses. As one person shares with another the most delicate and personal of experiences, a mutual trust and closeness inevitably develops. This is one of the most beautiful facets of spiritual direction, and it serves to enrich both parties' appreciation of their humanity. But in some cases this intimacy can also create complications. Directors who have problems with such close relationships—perhaps fearing their own vulnerability—may unconsciously retreat from the directee's opening heart. This is especially likely if sexual fears are involved.

No matter how comfortable one may be with intimacy it is sometimes difficult to maintain the vision that interpersonal intimacy in spiritual direction must serve to facilitate the directee's relationship with God. Interpersonal intimacy almost invariably leads to personal importance, and this can easily get in the way of attention towards the divine. But to pull away from intimacy is no answer. Instead, one must constantly be rechecking the openness of one's attention. If the interpersonal drama begins to interfere with this, it is time to take stock of what is happening. It may be necessary to pray about this and to encourage special relaxation and openness with that particular directee. Occasionally, especially if it is obvious that the relationship is becoming increasingly heavy for both parties, the director and directee need to talk it over openly and frankly together.

If awareness is not being noticed sufficiently to recognize these developments, several things may happen. The directee may become increasingly and unknowingly dependent on the director. There may be a push for more frequent or longer meetings. Telephone calls and meetings outside the direction hour may increase. If the director is blind to these changes, direction can be seriously hampered. On the other hand, the director may become increasingly preoccupied with or attracted to the directee. Here, it is the directee who must be on top of things, or the same kinds of distortion may happen.

It is also possible in such situations for the direction to develop an increasing mutuality. As I have said, this is not necessarily destructive in and of itself, but it does easily lead to casual conversation rather than true spiritual guidance. It can even lead to a role-reversal. One person gave an account of such a change with her spiritual director:

When we began in direction, I would go in every other week and we'd pray together and she'd ask me about my prayer life and I'd share my experiences. At times she would share some of her own experiences that related to mine. This was very helpful at the beginning, but over a period of several months she started sharing more and more of her own journey, and while I was interested, it often didn't seem like she was really addressing herself to my situation. She seemed to look at it as if we were on a journey together, and we were both searching along similar paths. I think I became trapped into this for a while; I was helping her and she was helping me. But more recently, it actually seems that I'm being more of a director for her than she is for me. I don't think I'm really getting any spiritual direction anymore, and she thinks everything's fine.

This woman had been reluctant to discuss matters with her director, even though she had felt increasingly uneasy over the past several months. Finally however, she decided to broach the topic. The director was able to recognize and acknowledge the changes that had taken place in the relationship, but could not comfortably return to the more formal structure. The change had been going on for too long, and it seemed impossible to go back. They agreed to keep meeting as spiritual friends because they enjoyed each other's company, but the directee sought out another director.

While increasing dependency, mutuality, and role-reversal can occur as human psychological phenomena in any ongoing relationship, there is often more drive towards such aberrations in spiritual direction. This is because spiritual growth implies a lessening of self-concern in conjunction with deepening awareness of God. Because this sacrifice of self-importance is often too great to be accepted easily, people often strive to substitute relationships with each other for the most threatening parts of their relationship with God. This is another way of trying to have one's cake and eat it too—to experience belonging, love, and acceptance without having to sacrifice any cherished aspects of self-image. In becoming dependent upon one's spiritual director, one can avoid the deeper levels of one's utter dependency upon God. In increasing the importance of the spiritual direction relationship, it is possible to evade the most threatening realizations of how fiercely important one's relationship to God truly is. Fostering a mutuality in spiritual direction may allow for less accountability, confrontation, and critique. Reversal of roles carries this to its extreme. Both director and directee are often involved in these kinds of unconscious pitfalls; there can be no expectation that the director will have an easier time at surrender than the directee. Finally, it should be mentioned that a psychologically determined *unimportance* of the direction relationship can be used as spiritual avoidance. This is especially common in religious communities or other settings where one might have been in direction for years and be able to "go through the motions" without anything really happening. In such cases, direction becomes a mechanical act, essentially devoid of meaning or impact.

Sexual Feelings in Direction

There is perhaps no more obvious example of unconscious evasion of spiritual truth than the arousal of sexual feelings between director and directee.[2] This is not to say that such feelings cannot occur in a perfectly normal manner, arising from physical attraction as they might in any ongoing relationship. But more often than not, there are deeper factors involved. I am convinced that sexual feelings occur with at least as much frequency in spiritual direction as in counseling or psychotherapy relationships, and—as in psychotherapy—these feelings sometimes grow into infatuations and actual liaisons.

There are a number of reasons for this. Since the level of intimacy and the degree of vulnerability required for spiritual direction is so great—in fact greater than that of any therapeutic relationship—and so many inner feelings are liberated and shared, it is not surprising that some sexual feelings emerge and find an object in the person of the director. It is not uncommon for directees to announce, "I've never spoken about this to anyone but you," or to reflect, "I think you are the only person who really understands this deepest part of me." In such closeness, erotic feelings easily undergo the psychological mechanism of *condensation,* they coalesce with related feelings of intimacy and affection, and find a convenient focus upon the director as object.

Similarly, the director's own sexuality may be aroused by the closeness of the relationship and the vulnerability of the directee. Such feelings are so natural and so spontaneous that it must be assumed that some such feelings exist, at least unconsciously, in every spiritual relationship that has sufficient closeness to warrant the name of direction. For the most part, these feelings remain unconscious; they are effectively repressed and present no difficulty.[3] And in those instances where some such feelings do surface into awareness, most people are capable of acknowledging them for what they are and dealing with them lightly and appropriately.

But there are other unconscious sources that produce erotic feelings, and some of these may be more problematic. Sometimes sexual feelings are a manifestation of transference, representing some oedipal or dependency issue that is surfacing sexually. Here, the other signs of transference will be evident.

Another source of sexual feelings is related to power. It is a well-known psychological fact that of the various forces that may "condense" around sexuality, power is an especially common one. Some directees are sexually aroused by seeing themselves in a submissive relationship to the director. One man said, for example, "I gave my soul into her hands; how could I fail to love her?" Some directors have exploited the vulnerability of their directees for their own sexual titillation. Whether this occurs consciously or unconsciously, it can develop into a Svengali-like relationship in which the director seems to hold special mystical powers over the directee. The sexual undertones of this are obvious. The Jungian archetypes associated with spiritual directors include images of the mystical wizard or sorcerer—male or female—who penetrates with insight and controls with esoteric spiritual and sexual powers. Such images do indeed lurk in the unconscious dimensions of our minds, and they can influence behavior in very destructive ways.

It has long been noted that the process of spiritual awakening and growth is associated with periods of rising sexual passion. In part this comes from the frank liberation of energy that accompanies lessening of attachments and release of psychological blocks. It is also connected with the awakening of ever deeper levels of love. Often these energies surface as passionate feelings that seem to be looking for an object. It is all well and good to say that their true object is God, but pilgrims who find themselves suddenly infused with passion may have difficulty seeing God as a sufficiently identifiable, immediate, and substantial object. Instead, they may seek outlets for these feelings in sexual relationships with other people. Sometimes the other person is the director. Here, the essential situation is that of tremendous loving energy surfacing with no immediate place to go. If this can be recognized, the directee can often be helped to remain with this powerful energy in its open, vital form without having to condense it upon some specific object. The director needs to be especially cognizant of this loving energy as regards any specifically sexual feelings that arise within the directee; the directee may feel guilty about something that is really a graced flowering of spiritual potential that should be celebrated rather than denied or suppressed.

Sexual feelings may also occur within the direction relationship as an outright substitute (displacement) for one's hunger for the Lord. Here again, the desire for losing oneself in God often finds expression in the safer, less demanding act of giving oneself to another person. While seeking spiritual fulfillment in erotic sexual relationships is an exceedingly common phenomenon because it preserves self-image, it is never finally satisfying because it always represents a side-tracking of one's primary longing. This is not to say that normal sexual relationships need to interfere with one's search for God. They can, under the proper circumstances and with the right attitudes, be ways of celebrating God. And they can certainly be avenues towards deeper appreciation of oneself and others. Finally, they can be simple, honest expressions of our graced human existence. But they must be recognized for what they are—interpersonal relationships, and nothing more. When they become mixed up with more specifically spiritual aspirations, deep confusion can occur; celebrations of God's creation and searching for deeper relationship *with* God are not quite the same thing.

Most often, this mix-up occurs unconsciously, as an attempt to find fulfillment without ego sacrifice. The "fusion" (Fromm's term) of erotic experience feels more attractive and less threatening than the "union" of spirituality, which demands ultimate self-sacrifice. But in recent years this kind of confusion has been deepened by a number of publications, workshops, and seminars of the pop–psycho/spiritual/sexuality genre that support the notion that sexual intercourse is an excellent way of *finding* God. I do not know whether the leadership of such enterprises consciously exploits the confusions of sexuality and spirituality or not. But I do know a number of people who have been wounded by such experiences. In order to avoid any misunderstanding here, I must re-emphasize that a full integration of sexuality is an essential component of our overall spiritual growth. Our essences, our souls, *are* sexual, and we reduce our God-given reality if we deny or devalue the sexual dimensions of ourselves. But to focus on this one dimension as the way to God is to deny both the terror and the wonder of our true wholeness in God.

Ironically, the promulgation of sex-as-the-way-to-God usually occurs in the context of "holistic" movements.[4] Because a holistic approach allows one to deal with sexuality in the context of spiritual growth (which I think is appropriate), it can also allow one to reduce spirituality to a limited sexual enterprise (which clearly is not appropriate). It is very pleasing to the mind to consider our incarnational qualities in an attitude of wholeness that includes psychology, sexuality, body, work, relationship, and all other aspects of life. It is good to recognize that we are many-faceted gems. It is consoling to associate wholeness of body and mind with wholeness of spirit. And it is joyous to see the work of God in every aspect of ourselves, in each other, and in the world around us. Certainly these understandings are more accurate and efficient than some of the older ways that saw flesh as the eternal enemy of spirit. As long as we are in the business of enjoying God's creation, celebrating God's work, and appreciating God's love, our attitudes of wholeness do nothing but serve us well. But in the conscious or unconscious search for God, in our struggle to appease that deep aching hunger for a fuller realization of God, we must take care. Here it is all too easy to use our newfound ability to affirm every aspect of ourselves as a way to become preoccupied with only one aspect of ourselves. This is how wholeness turns into reduction, how in the guise of celebrating one dimension of God's creation we unknowingly begin to worship that creation instead of God.

In the midst of appreciating and enjoying the wonder of God's creation, it is essential to at least try to see through that wonder, through all of its beauty and tragedy and pleasure and pain, through all of our images and sensations and intensities to the incomprehensible, mysterious truth of the Creator. It seems to me that at our present place in history, the two most important dimensions of life to see *through* are psychology and sexuality. Both provide endless opportunities for reducing or eclipsing the reality of God for us as we delude ourselves into believing we see the Creator when we are really viewing the creation. They are dangerous in this respect precisely because they are so wonderful, so fundamentally good. Our individual and collective minds are an exceedingly rich resource for exploration of ourselves as God's creation. But while the mind is *of* God, it is not God in God's entirety. Sexuality offers us the closest possible experience of joining with another, and it reflects in broken but endlessly hopeful ways what God's inloveness with us might be like. But it is not the path *to* God.

Dealing with Sexuality in Direction

As we have seen, sexual feelings can surface in spiritual direction in a variety of forms and for a number of reasons. Because of historic taboos, directors and directees alike may find themselves reluctant to face these issues openly. While it is certainly neither necessary nor helpful to adopt the old psychoanalytic cliche of "looking for sex in everything," spiritual directors do need to be as open and receptive to this material as possible. In this regard it may be helpful for the director to ask a few questions about sexuality early on in the relationship. As well as providing useful information, this gets the issue of sexuality out in the open and identifies it as an acceptable topic for discussion. Then the directee may feel more at ease in bringing up sexual material later on as needed. In exploring a directee's prayer life in an early session, for example, the director might ask Have you ever had any other imagery or strong feelings in prayer? Any strong emotions of love, body sensations, or sexual images? What are the times you've felt closest to God? What about nature, music, sex, worship, or times of crisis?

Sexual sensations and images occur with considerable frequency in prayer, though sometimes they are denied or quickly repressed. If they are allowed into full awareness, they may be a strong source of guilt or shame for some people or a source of distracting fascination for others. If a directee can share these experiences openly in direction, it may be possible for the director to point out that they are indeed images and sensations, just like the host of other perceptions we may encounter. Further, they may have considerable symbolic value in reflecting the depth of our passion for God or of God's passion for us. Whether such phenomena are initially seen as especially good or bad, they really constitute problems only if they are taken too seriously for too long and become a source of exclusive preoccupation.

If from time to time the director asks how the directee feels about the relationship, or if "evaluation times" are scheduled regularly, there will be opportunity to mutually explore any changes or strong feelings of a sexual nature—or anything else for that matter—that may be affecting the relationship. Such periodic evaluations, either prescheduled or spontaneously initiated, are very helpful beyond the issue of dealing with sexuality. They are opportunities for raising important questions, desires or concerns that might not otherwise surface. I feel they should be a part of every direction relationship as a matter of course.

All the while, it is important for the director to be cognizant of the more subtle phenomena that may signal that the relationship with a specific directee is becoming especially important. If a directee appears in a dream, comes to prominence or is forgotten in prayer, or keeps arising in one's thoughts, it is worth taking a look at the relationship. Similarly, feelings of confusion and uneasiness during the direction sessions should prompt an examination. The fact that some of these experiences may have sexual qualities need be no cause for special alarm. To know this simply adds to one's ability to appraise what is happening more accurately. Directors should first reflect prayerfully on these issues themselves, then perhaps discuss them with their own directors or colleagues, and then raise them or not for open evaluation with the directee.

It must be re-emphasized here that although objective analysis and psychological examination can help clarify what is going on, these should be supplements, never substitutes, for the more traditional discernments of the spiritual life and the personal prayer and meditation of the spiritual director. These latter elements remain the bulwark of discrimination in spiritual direction, and if they are forsaken in the name of psychodynamic analysis, spiritual direction will cease and some confused amalgamation of psychology in spiritual trappings will take its place.

Once it has been identified that sexual issues are arising in spiritual direction, it should rapidly become clear whether they constitute a problem or not. Inevitably this has to do with whether these issues—regardless of their form or strength—support, hinder, or have no effect upon attentiveness and openness towards God's work in the directee. It is entirely possible for manifestations of sexuality to occur without any real relevance whatsoever to spiritual direction. This is especially likely if the directee is mature in sexual attitudes and integration, and is neither restricted by guilt nor confused about the differences between erotic love for others and passionate love for God.

Similarly, sexual feelings can be very helpful and supportive in spiritual growth if they are seen as representations and specifically channeled expressions of basic spiritual energy. Here again, however, it is necessary to recognize sexuality as a specific and bounded human phenomenon that, apart from its procreative, celebrative, and communicative purposes, is at best a symbol of the endlessly pervasive and boundless love of God.

If this recognition is not clear, as is the case with most of us at one time or another, sexuality can present a problem for spiritual growth. It is at such times that one may mistake interpersonal eroticism for spiritual exploration or substitute another person for God as the object of one's ultimate concern. And as we have seen, there are occasions when this other person happens to be one's spiritual director or directee.

It is confusing enough when a directee falls into romantic love with the director, but more troublesome when a director becomes infatuated with a directee. It is still more difficult when the experience is mutual. In all of these instances things can be vastly improved if the situation is recognized, acknowledged, and discussed openly. But this is often not what happens. Sometimes the directee will be so sexually guilt-ridden and inhibited that only the most subtle and indirect expressions of erotic love can be permitted, and the truth of the matter must remain unconscious. Perhaps the director will also be guilt-ridden and inhibited, denying his or her own sexuality and refusing to deal with that of the directee.

While it might be hoped that spiritual directors would be more open and mature than this, many are not. For example, one woman spiritual director consistently refused to accept the obvious fact that one of her male directees had fallen in love with her. This went on for months, during which most of the direction sessions were spent talking about the relationship in such disguised ways that little spiritual direction could actually take place. When out of desperation the directee finally declared his love openly, the director immediately terminated the relationship. In processing this at a later date, the director was able to examine some of her own "baggage" associated with sexuality and felt more capable of dealing with it in her directees. But as grace would have it, she then experienced an even more threatening situation when one of her female directees expressed a sexual attraction for her. She felt exquisitely anxious, but this time sought some supervision and was finally able to deal with the matter so that direction could continue in a productive and very helpful way.

In another example, a Protestant clergyman confided that when a married female directee expressed attraction to him, his first response was to try to get her to go to marriage counseling with her husband. As well as being personally threatened by this attraction, the director was somewhat ignorant concerning sexual matters. He assumed that if a marriage was adequate, neither partner would experience attractions to other people. After some reflection, he also acknowledged some sexual stereotyping in feeling that while a husband might experience such attractions, a wife never would unless there were something seriously defective in the marriage or in her personality. In this case also, the direction relationship was terminated, with the directee going on to a better relationship and the director embarking on his own slow but rewarding journey towards sexual understanding and integration.

Sometimes, as we have mentioned, a director will experience erotic attraction towards a directee. Whether this occurs in a same-sex or an opposite-sex relationship, it need not necessarily disrupt the direction. But it is critically important that the director examine the feelings very carefully, attempting to identify the precise nature of the attraction and its potential effects upon the relationship. In prayer and reflection, the director should seek answers to such questions as: Is this primarily a physical attraction? What is it, precisely, about him or her that I find so appealing? Is it something in his or her personality? Am I intrigued by the directee's inner life or experience? Am I perhaps distorting my own compassion, or displacing my love for God? Is it possible that I might be seduced by my own power over this person? How does this situation relate to my past sexual history and present fantasies? Is there some kind of parent/child feeling going on? Where does my curiosity lie in this, and what most intrigues me?

Then some questions about the relationship itself and its impact on spiritual awareness should be asked. In what ways might I be *using* this directee? How easily could I let him or her go if I determine that it's necessary? How comfortable does the directee feel with me? Are my feelings in any way having an impact on the directee's prayer life or awareness? How does his or her importance to me affect my own moment-by-moment attention to God in the meetings and in my daily life? Am I serving God, the directee, or myself in this? Can I deal with these feelings and desires openly and freely? Can I let them be in my awareness and offer them to God, or will I be compelled either to suppress them or act on them in some way? Can I see them rising and falling like other thoughts and sensations, or do they capture me? How does all of this affect my surrender?

In most cases it is necessary for the director to discuss these feelings with someone else to ensure some objectivity and perspective. It is nearly always possible to do this without jeopardizing confidentiality. In addition, it may be helpful to do some journal work or exploration of one's dreams or both. And always the matter should be taken to prayer. Finally, if it is decided that the feelings are strong enough to have some kind of real impact on the direction itself, they should be discussed with the directee. It is most especially important to be frank and open about this if one is contemplating a termination of the direction relationship. If some other excuse is dreamed up, the directee is likely to feel confused, rejected, or otherwise destructively misled.

There are two exceptions to the rule of open discussion of these matters with the directee. First, the discussion may be postponed if it is clear that the attraction is light, mild, and in no way disturbing to one's awareness or to the relationship itself. This postponement, however, must not involve "forgetting" the issue. One does need to stay awake to it. Second, the topic may be avoided if it is absolutely certain that discussing it would be harmful to the directee. The first exception may occur rather frequently; the second only with extreme rarity.

When the attraction is mutual, an up-front and open discussion is mandatory. The kinds of questions raised above should then be processed together as well as individually. In many cases this can be accomplished lightly and without taking too much time or energy from the process of ongoing direction. Often it may provide a rich focus for exploring the relationship between human and divine loving. Occasionally, sensations of affection for the other person can be utilized as signals to redirect one's attention towards the divine, and the energy of attraction can be channeled into more panoramic and less singular loving.

At other times, when the attraction is accompanied by strong attachment and importance, it may be impossible to deal with things lightly. Here there may need to be an acknowledgment of the attachment and an attempt to accept the pain that goes with it. While previously we were talking about an acceptance and allowing of the attraction, we are now at the level of having to accept and allow the suffering of unrequited erotic passion. This too can be a source of energy and insight, but it takes more discipline and requires more constant attentiveness.

If even this cannot be achieved, and the attachment remains so strong that it monopolizes one's attention or seeks satisfaction so strongly that it is a constant discomfort, one may indeed have to terminate the relationship. It is by no means the end of the world if this has to happen, but it is important that the situation be handled honestly and the decision be made together if at all possible. Even in cases of mutual attraction it is likely that one party will be able to handle it more comfortably than the other. It is very appropriate for this to be acknowledged, and it need not interfere with mutuality in deciding about termination.

Under no circumstances, I feel, can effective spiritual direction go on in a relationship that has been genitalized. I am aware that there are some modern writers and thinkers who maintain that this can happen, but I have never heard of a case where intercourse proved to be anything other than a serious disruption to direction in the long run. More, it is almost certain to be wounding to the hearts and souls of both parties. Erotic sexuality simply provides too many opportunities for psychological defensiveness and avoidance of spiritual truth for it to be effectively incorporated into spiritual direction, even if one were to overlook the moral implications.

It is my opinion that even in marriage the sexual and relational overtones are so strong and importance-producing that spouses cannot be effective spiritual directors for each other. They can be spiritual friends, spiritual compatriots; they can support each other and even share a mutual journey in many respects. But there is neither sufficient perspective nor adequate freedom of attentiveness for one to be director to the other. I say this with full knowledge that in some modern fundamentalist circles wives are told that only their husbands should be their spiritual directors. It is my belief that marriage relationships are simply too loaded with other psychological issues to allow for free and effective direction. As partial support for this, it can be noted that in our modern society is is only in exceptional marriages that husband and wife can even share their spiritual journeys, much less guide one another. The far more common pattern is for one spouse to be somewhat threatened by, or at best distantly supportive of, the other's journey. There may be respect for each other's pilgrimages, but often there is little in the way of full understanding.

It is hoped that this might change as our culture becomes more comfortable with human spirituality and more at ease with equal power and competence of men and women. This will, with grace, allow people's spiritual journeys to be more openly shared and less threatening. But even so, I doubt there will come a time when spouses can generally fill the role of true spiritual directors for each other. I know one couple who share their spiritual journey very deeply and see it as a common enterprise. They meet with their spiritual director together, and they also offer spiritual direction as a couple. This is an exciting and very hopeful experiment, and thus far their endeavors show great promise. But they too are aware of the special gift of their relationship, and they do not act as directors for each other except in the most transient and informal of ways.

A strong case can be made that spiritual directors should have very limited relationships with their directees outside of the direction relationship. For example, novice masters in religious communities cannot easily be directors for their students because their positions of authority impede freedom of interchange. Similarly, it would be difficult in most cases to seek spiritual direction from one's boss or subordinates in business. As in marriage, the emotional importance of such relationships would generally load spiritual direction with extraneous agendas and cause distraction and loss of perspective. Still, such decisions must be made individually. In some cases, contact outside the direction sessions can actually enhance direction if it supports friendship without stimulating importance or heaviness.

Here again, it is important to keep clear the distinctions between informal spiritual friendships and formal spiritual direction. While a certain perspective and "purity" of relationship must be protected in formal spiritual direction in order to minimize unconscious psychological distortions, the informal ways in which we can support and nurture each other's spiritual growth and be instruments of grace for each other are literally endless. We can, at least theoretically, be spiritual friends with anyone.

7. Disorder: Psychiatric Syndromes

One of the more common concerns encountered by spiritual directors is the possibility of significant emotional or mental disorder in a directee. There was a time when many spiritual directors either had no great knowledge of psychology or simply did not believe in it. While this meant that they often missed psychopathology and failed to integrate spiritual and psychological concerns, they also were spared considerable and often needless worry about the directee's going crazy, and they were able to avoid the pitfall of psychologizing the process of spiritual direction.

That time is gone. Nowadays nearly everyone who offers formal spiritual direction has enough knowledge of psychology to feel intimidated. And while this can lead to a more integrated view of the full human person, it may also result in a devaluation of more clearly "spiritual" insights. Even more dangerously, a preoccupation with psychodynamics sometimes reduces the entire process of spiritual guidance to a kind of "psycho-curiosity" that avoids any real confrontation with the transcendent dimensions of life.[1]

During the Second World War, in large part due to the contributions of W. C. Menninger, psychiatry became a legitimate component of the military health care system. The result was an invaluable reduction in misery and disability, in many cases actually lifesaving. But to the military in the 1940s it sometimes seemed that the effect of this mental health movement was to find psychiatric problems where none had previously existed. As one disgruntled officer said, "We didn't have any mental illness in the Army until you psychiatrists showed up!"

Many people tend to share this officer's sentiments. There is a kind of revulsion at the degree to which psychiatry labels people. It can cause no little rancor to see a hard-working and dedicated person diagnosed as "obsessive" or a sweet, unassuming one called "passive dependent." We really would rather see ourselves as being inspired and aspiring rather than driven by "unconscious forces." And it would be much nicer to believe that we marry our spouses or choose our faiths out of our own free volition rather than as a result of "psychological determinants."

As in most things, some kind of middle ground needs to be found here. The behavioral sciences have established beyond doubt that unconscious psychological and biological forces do indeed influence our behavior. But we also have some freedom of choice, and the more we understand our unconscious "determinants" the more we may be free of them. Similarly, the labels with which psychiatry categorizes mental conditions have a degree of validity that— though always relative—is undeniable. It would be helpful, I think, to recognize that these labels are in many ways quite accurate, but that they are also just labels. They reveal something about the attributes, but nothing of the essence, of a person. They describe certain characteristics and conditions, but they do not really address the soul.

For a reasonably balanced perspective in this arena, spiritual directors should be familiar with two basic psychiatric understandings. The first of these is *personality theory*. This includes a variety of hypotheses dealing with how human personality is formed, the factors that contribute to its development, and the stages through which it seems to grow. There are several good books (such as Brenner and Erikson) that describe such theories in understandable terms. I shall not attempt to address these here, except to say that nearly all such theories maintain these assumptions: personality is in large part determined by a combination of early genetic, physical, and experiential factors; it goes through a number of stages, each of which is affected by the ones that have preceded it; and adjustment in later life is determined by how the personality responds or reacts to the experiences and encounters of life. It must also be understood that at the time of this writing there is no psychiatrically accepted personality theory that includes any real consideration of grace or of transcendence.[2]

The second aspect of psychiatric understanding is that of the diagnostic categories themselves, the labels and descriptions given for psychiatric disorders, along with something of their causes and treatments. An understanding of both of these bodies of knowledge is helpful more for appreciating a person's condition than for comprehending it. We can more intimately address a person's spiritual needs if we understand something about how personality develops and what can go wrong with it. But this is not the same thing as labeling the person. In this regard, it may be valuable to reconsider the modern differences that exist between discernment and diagnosis.

Discernment and Diagnosis

"Discernment" (or the Greek *diakrisis)* refers to an act of separating apart. "Diagnosis" refers to distinguishing through knowledge. The etymology is as follows: *discernment* and *diakrisis* have the roots *dis/dia* (apart) and *cernere/krisis* (to separate). The word *discretio,* used by St. Benedict and many others, is the past participle of *discernere. Diagnosis,* in Greek, refers to "through knowledge" or even "thorough knowledge," emphasizing knowledge or even authoritarian judgment (c.f. Acts 25:21, the diagnosis of the emperor). I have previously indicated that diagnosis looks to label disorder so that it can be corrected, but discernment seeks to discriminate among inclinations so that a proper direction can be followed. Now, with the understanding that knowledge is such a major component of diagnosis, the differences become even clearer. To make a diagnosis, a person must rely very heavily on the memorization and logical classification of numerous signs and symptoms and then use an extensive process of both inductive and deductive reasoning. This emphasis on personal knowledge and rational capacity accentuates subject/object distinctions. I, the knowledgable subject, diagnose you, the object of my examination. In medical and psychiatric practice it is assumed that intimacy will interfere with this objectivity and impair the logical processing required for effective diagnosis. While there remain some physicians who still look upon diagnosis as an art, the overall thrust of medical science would hold that, given sufficient information, the best diagnoses would be made by computers.

Discernment, however, is generally seen as more of a gifted process than diagnosis, a graced charism that happens *through* the director. Intuitive senses are seen as more significant, and intimacy—albeit without attachment—is necessary rather than problematic. Too much subject/object distinction, "objectivity," ruins the process of discernment, just as too little ruins diagnosis. As Teresa of Avila maintains, however, knowledge should not be *underemphasized* in discernment. In her *Life* she went so far as to indicate that non-"spiritual" persons with sufficient knowledge would make better directors than "spiritual" persons without knowledge. (The historical context in which she said this is important for an adequate interpretation of her meaning.)

Further, discernments do not usually come up with labels, but with sharp insights into the nature of things. This is certainly true for the best kinds of diagnoses as well. Karl Menninger has long tried to convince the psychiatric world that real diagnosis is a matter of understanding rather than labeling, but the fact of the matter is that the majority of psychiatric practitioners give precedence to labeling over insight when it comes to diagnosis. In contrast, the deepest discernments cannot be labeled at all; often they cannot even be put into words. Instead, they comprise shared subtle senses of spiritual movements, seen clearly, but often too numinous to objectify. Essentially, diagnosis seeks solutions to mystery in order to destroy it. Discernment seeks a discriminating appreciation of mystery, in order to respond to it in accordance with God's will.

Psychiatric Labeling

The psychiatric labeling of mental disorders has two primary facets. First is the attempt to name syndromes and diseases as accurately and clearly as possible. This is called nomenclature. Second, there is an endeavor to categorize and classify the disorders into an organizational structure that will be logically coherent for the purposes of diagnosis and treatment. This is called nosology.

Through the years, the American Psychiatric Association, the World Health Organization, the National Institutes of Mental Health, and a number of other agencies have worked out a series of systems of nosology and nomenclature for mental disorders. For the United States, this has resulted in three editions of a *Diagnostic and Statistical Manual,* each of which has supplanted an earlier in an attempt to provide a more accurate and a more consensual basis for diagnosis. The most recent of these, popularly referred to as *DSM-III*, was published in 1980.[3] It represented a major re-ordering and renaming of psychiatric disorders and included possibilities for appraising such factors as pre-existing personality structures, precipitating stresses, and degrees of impairment.

DSM-III is a much more sophisticated and comprehensive system than any of those that preceded it, and considerable conflict surrounded its design and implementation. Some behavioral scientists are enthralled with its coherent organization; most of it can even be computerized. Others feel it is misleading in its sophistication, making the disorders sound like actual and definitively established diseases, when in fact many are nothing more than culturally determined descriptions of symptoms for which the causes are extremely unclear.

Both sides have a case here. The structure of *DSM-III* is invaluable for research, and should provide for a much greater diagnostic reliability (agreement) than any prior system. But as with the prior manuals, many of the "disorders" actually do consist simply of symptom descriptions, revealing our lack of understanding of the true nature and origin of a great number of psychiatric "illnesses." It would be a mistake to assume, for example, that schizophrenia is a disease as specific as smallpox or cholera. The best modern understandings of schizophrenia are that it has a "multifactorial causation" (a number of causes) and that it probably represents a collection of different disorders that simply have a few symptoms in common. Such symptom collections are called "syndromes."

It must also be admitted that some of the diagnoses are indeed culturally determined. As but one example, there was a great turmoil about whether or not to call homosexuality a psychiatric disorder. It has been so labeled in some previous systems, but there was a strong movement to have it deleted entirely from the new classification. The final decision was to include only a category of "ego-dystonic" homosexuality, indicating that it is only a disorder when the individual experiences it as such (wants to perform heterosexually but cannot). Other sexual proclivities, some personality disorders, and an occasional dissociative disorder might not be seen as pathological in certain other cultures. Still, most of the major diagnoses (the schizophrenias, affective disorders, and organic problems) are cross-culturally valid.

One of the more striking changes in *DSM-III* was the deletion of the overall category of neurosis. It was found that the variety of symptoms identifiable as neurotic could not validly be grouped together. In addition, there were considerable difficulties in agreeing upon a definition of neurosis. For years, neuroses were popularly assumed to be of purely psychodynamic origin. But even Freud intimated a belief in genetic or physical causation behind the psychodynamics. Later, behaviorists held neurotic problems to be learned responses to internal and external stimuli. Still more recently, some supposedly neurotic difficulties have been shown to respond dramatically to medication. Antidepressants, for example, have proven amazingly helpful in many cases of phobia. This has caused further doubt as to the purely psychological causation of neurosis.

This brings us to a final observation that must be made concerning popular psychiatric thinking. The discoveries of new chemical treatments for psychiatric disorders are often accompanied by rapid shifts in assumptions as to the causes of the disorders. For example, the discovery in the 1950s that many schizophrenic symptoms could be alleviated by certain chemicals led to a widespread belief that schizophrenia must therefore be a physical illness. A similar, but even more striking, shift occurred in the case of manic depressive illness (now called bipolar affective disorder) with the discovery of lithium carbonate treatment. While some genetic propensities had been identified in this disorder because of its occurrence in family members, tremendous study had also gone into attempting to identify psychodynamic and sociocultural causes. But when it was established that lithium carbonate was essentially curative in many cases, a large number of psychiatrists immediately assumed that the illness was wholly physical in nature. Similar shifts are now going on in the theories concerning milder depressions, which have been increasingly associated with brain chemical changes. The overriding assumption in all this is that if a condition can be identified as associated with brain chemical changes, if it responds dramatically to chemical treatment, or both, the underlying causative problem must be of a chemical nature. Although this reasoning is by itself very simplistic, a large number of psychiatrists have fallen prey to it. Some say, for example, that within a few years psychiatry will cease to exist as a medical discipline because all psychiatric problems will be found to have neurological origins.

As mentioned in Chapter 2, the fact that certain psychological manifestations are mediated by brain chemicals or may be strongly affected by administered drugs does not necessarily mean that thoughts, feelings, or moods are *created* by chemicals. Just as thoughts, feelings, memories, and behavior can be triggered by certain concentrations and combinations of brain chemicals, so also can thoughts, feelings, and the like trigger changes in chemicals. At the most basic level, a level that science is just beginning to address, the human being is such an intimate joining of mind/brain/body/spirit/energy/consciousness that all arbitrary separations must be fundamentally inaccurate.

With this in mind, we can proceed to examine some of the psychiatric disorders that might be encountered in or have relevance to spiritual direction. Please refrain from trying to diagnose yourself or anyone else, for the information here is not adequate to accomplish this. My suggestion is simply to read through the material and let yourself grasp its "gestalt," its overall themes and structure. This will provide sufficient grounding and perspective to serve well in spiritual direction situations. A number of categories are included in *DSM-III* that bear little relevance to spiritual direction. I will note the major ones in order to preserve the overall structure of the nomenclature, but will keep their descriptions severely condensed.

Disorders Usually First Identified in Childhood

Few of these disorders are relevant to spiritual direction. The most significant is *mental retardation*, essentially defined as a score of below 70 on standard I.Q. tests. Also included are disorders of attention, conduct, eating, and movement and other physical syndromes such as stuttering, bedwetting, sleepwalking, and others.

Organic Mental Disorders

Organic mental disorders are problems that can be definitely associated with some organic or chemical change within the brain, and in which the physical change is the cause of the symptoms. A number of these disorders may be pertinent to spiritual direction. Included are the *dementias,* which are associated with such causes as senility, arteriosclerosis (hardening of the arteries), or traumatic injury. Symptoms of dementia include a weakening of memory (with memory for recent events usually being more impaired than for remote events), difficulty with abstract thinking, decreasing impulse control, and perhaps a reoccurrence of childlike behavior and mood swings. Dementias are generally characterized by progressive deterioration unless the underlying physical cause is treatable.

Related, but with different causes, are the deliria and intoxications, which may include some of the symptoms of dementia, but are also generally associated with a marked alteration of awareness or attention. A person with dementia is alert to the environment yet confused by it, but one with delirium or intoxication is often unable to attend to the environment at all because of a general clouding of consciousness or an exceedingly rapid shifting of attention. Often delirium is associated with *hallucinations* (perceiving things not there) or *illusions* (misinterpreting things that are there).

It might be said that dementia is an inability to process and integrate the contents of awareness effectively, while delirium is an aberration of the awareness itself. Generally, deliria are acute (short-lived), while dementias are chronic (long-lasting). While delirium is sometimes caused by injury or internal physical disease (high fever, for example), the most common forms are related to intoxication with or withdrawal from alcohol or other drugs. An extremely wide variety of chemicals can cause this, and usually the delirium itself improves when the chemical is fully removed from the system and one has adjusted to its absence. Long-term effects can persist in a number of ways, however. Alcohol and other chemicals interfere with brain metabolism and can actually destroy brain cells. This can lead to chronic dementia. Treatment of deliria and intoxications consists of protecting the person while the offending substance is removed or the physical condition corrected. A few dementias can be helped in this way also, but many are essentially irreversible.

The dementias that occur with old age are primarily signaled by severe impairment of memory and regression to childlike emotional changes. But sometimes depression or paranoid concerns may be early symptoms. More importantly, people sometimes mistake pure depression in an older person for dementia. This happens so commonly that the condition has been unofficially labeled "pseudodementia." Treatable disorders such as this should always be considered lest someone by tragically written off as "just senile."

Deterioration of memory or attention-focusing capacity can sometimes be disturbing in prayer when certain "abilities" to concentrate or remain centered are noted to be lacking. People can be considerably helped with this through re-affirmation that the quality of prayer is never determined by one's abilities, but rather by the graced willingness to depend upon the Lord and to allow the Spirit to pray within oneself as It will. On very rare occasions deleria may be associated with extremes of ascetical practice, such as extensive fasting or sensory deprivations, but standard discernments should make these differentiations clear.

Substance Use Disorders

The misuse of chemicals is one of the most prevalent conditions in our society. Over nine million men and women suffer from alcoholism, and millions more depend upon tranquilizers for getting through the day, sedatives for sleeping at night, stimulants for losing weight or staying alert, cocaine or marijuana for "relaxation." It is estimated that eight million Americans a year take Valium alone. And then of course there are always tobacco and caffeine.

In the *DSM-III* nomenclature a differentiation is made between *abuse* of a chemical—a prolonged use that impairs functioning—and *dependence,* which is heralded by the development of tolerance (needing increasing amounts to produce the same effect) or withdrawal symptoms when the use is stopped.

While alcoholism is not an official diagnosis in this classification, most authorities agree that alcoholism exists wherever there is either abuse or dependence. Thus it does not suffice for one to say "I am not an alcoholic because I can do without it." As long as a pattern of drinking is established that in any way interferes with social, vocational, or other functioning (and here I would include the spiritual dimension, as in interference with prayer or daily awareness) there is abuse, and thereby, alcoholism.

The term "addiction" is also not a diagnosis in this system, but it can be considered as essentially synonymous with dependence. It does not much matter whether withdrawal symptoms are primarily physical (chills, shaking, cramps, and the like) or psychological (irritability, agitation, restlessness, and so on). If the symptoms happen, dependence exists.

The treatment of chemical abuse and dependence is extremely difficult. Because of the strong behavioral conditioning process of taking-drug/feeling-good, feeling-bad/taking-drug/feeling-good is so powerful, and because the mind creates such inventive rationalizations and denials in order to perpetuate the pattern, one becomes less and less self-motivated or able to change the situation. In most instances, it is only when things get to some kind of "rock bottom" that change is possible, and then often only with considerable help, support, and grace.

It absolutely does not suffice to assume that one becomes dependent on a chemical because of underlying or pre-existing personality problems. The conditioning of the chemical usage is enough to create dependency without any pre-existing problems. Such problems may or may not be present, but until and unless the chemical use is stopped it is impossible to ascertain what, if anything, needs to be addressed at a psychological level. Thus, attempts to stop dependency through psychotherapy or self-understanding seldom work. Such endeavors have put the cart before the horse. The pattern of chemical abuse must be broken first; then psychotherapy may be in order.

Chemical abuse and dependency constitute for me the sacred illnesses of our time. In few other conditions does one come up so definitively against the fierce line between grace and personal will power. The agonizing cycles of willfulness and defeat that surround an addiction symbolize more than anything else our utter dependence upon, as A.A. puts it, a "higher power." In the 1981 ABC-TV documentary "The Monastery," a young monk refers to the "rock bottom" experience by saying that at such a point "it's either worship or suicide." He was not specifically referring to chemical abuse, but the "rock bottom" is the same regardless of how one gets there.

Schizophrenic Disorders

There probably is no such thing as "schizophrenia." Instead, the syndromes called by this name share a group of symptoms. There may be a variety of causes, and appropriate treatments may also vary.

At the outset it needs to be understood that schizophrenia does not refer to the hackneyed "split personality" in which two or more people seem to occupy the same body. (This, as we shall see, is an essentially unrelated dissociative disorder.) Instead, *schizophrenia* suggests a fragmentation or severe disorganization of psychological functioning. Thoughts do not connect well with each other, nor with feelings. Multiple thoughts and feelings may be experienced simultaneously and continuously in ways that make no sense and seem wholly unrelated to what is actually going on in life.

In contrast to dementia and delirium, memory is usually maintained and one can generally orient oneself in terms of time, geography, and other people. But the use of this information is seriously compromised because of the disorganization of thought processes. Sometimes several thoughts are experienced simultaneously, creating a "word salad" that is incomprehensible both subjectively and to others. At other times thoughts become "blocked," apparently stuck in upon each other so that they can neither be experienced nor expressed. Often the mood or feeling tone ("affect") seems to be incongruous to the words being spoken. Sometimes all evidence of mood disappears entirely and nothing is visible but a blank stare. This is said to be a "flat affect."

Other classic symptoms include delusions (fixed mistaken beliefs), especially those involving controlling or being controlled by others through mysterious means. Especially characteristic of schizophrenia is a belief that one's thoughts are being controlled, inserted or removed by someone else. Also common are hallucinations of voices that seem to control, influence, or judge one's mind. Occasionally one may "see things" (experience visual hallucinations), but this is more characteristic of organic delerium or intoxication than of schizophrenia.

Various constellations and arrangements of these symptoms produce the different categories of schizophrenia. If disordered movement is most prominent, such as statuelike immobility, bizarre posturing, or wild bodily outbursts, this may be *catatonic* schizophrenia. If disorganization of thinking and feeling is most outstanding, one might consider the label of *disorganized* schizophrenia (previously called hebephrenic). More commonly, delusions having to do with hostile intent are predominant, often with grandiosity (feelings of special personal power or greatness), and deep unwarranted fear of being done wrong by others. This constellation would probably be called *paranoid* schizophrenia. Still more frequently there is a mixture of these various symptoms, which is labeled as *undifferentiated* schizophrenia.

Religious hallucinations, delusions, and preoccupations have always been a frequent finding in schizophrenic disorders. Sometimes paranoid grandiosity—which is usually a compensation for a devastatingly negative self-image—includes identification of oneself as God, Jesus, Mary, or a special emissary thereof. At other times, a mystico-spiritual explanation is invented to account for the strange voices one hears and the bizarre experiences one undergoes. Since religion, at its core, defies traditional logical understanding, it is probably the most chosen arena for explaining illogical and incomprehensible phenomena. Finally, and I think most importantly, schizophrenia is characterized by frequent and flagrant failures of repression. The most basic and fundamental urges of humankind are expressed blatantly and with startling crudity when schizophrenia destroys the natural defenses. Since spiritual hunger is perhaps the most basic of these urges, it is only natural that it should appear in very rude form along with primitive extremes of sexuality, aggression, and the like.

As I have indicated earlier, it usually does not take much psychiatric sophistication to distinguish between schizophrenic religiosity and legitimate spiritual experience. The simplest of classic discernment methods, combined with basic common sense, will generally suffice.[4] But it does need to be remembered that the schizophrenic disorders are major, deep, and pervasive, affecting a variety of functions and interfering with many areas of a person's mind and life. Further, this deterioration in functioning is not a brief, transient disturbance. *DSM-III* states that signs of the disturbance must last continuously for at least six months for the diagnosis of schizophrenia to be made. One weird experience or transient disturbance of thought does not make a diagnosis of schizophrenia.

The treatment of schizophrenic disorders is a focus for considerable debate. While most psychiatrists advocate using medication and supportive therapies to achieve as rapid an amelioration of symptoms as possible (the "seal it over" school), others say that a schizophrenic illness can be an existential or spiritual growth-experience and recommend limited use of medicine and lots of time and insight-oriented attention (the "work it through" school). For what it is worth, my impression is that "working it through" is possible only in extremely unusual instances and may actually be harmful for many people.

I have never seen an individual who really came out "better" for having gone through a real schizophrenic illness, and usually the disorder wounds the person in terms of later functioning and self-image. For these and a variety of other more technical reasons, I strongly advocate that the major symptoms of any true schizophrenic disorder should be treated as rapidly and effectively as possible. Only then, if the condition permits and the person is willing, can an attempt be made to try to understand and integrate the deeper meanings of the experience. I feel this is most especially true for severe and acute schizophrenic conditions.

Most often, the treatment of schizophrenic disorders includes some form of *neuroleptic* medication. These drugs, which are also called "major tranquilizers" to distinguish them from minor anti-anxiety drugs such as Librium or Valium, affect the concentration and uptake of specific brain chemicals, like dopamine. This effect, which occurs primarily within the deep central areas of the brain where emotions are mediated, has a decided influence on the symptoms of many schizophrenic disorders. But the precise ways in which this happens are not yet fully understood, and the results are variable. For one person, a neuroleptic drug may seem truly "curative," while it may be of no value, or may even make things worse, for another. Often several different medications must be tried. All have potential for substantial side effects, but none is likely to produce dependence.

With medication, *supportive psychotherapy* is usually helpful. "Supportive" here refers to contacts that help the person handle daily-life tasks and stresses, and that encourage the re-establishment of defenses and understandable thinking. This is to be contrasted with *insight-oriented* or *dynamic therapy*, which seeks to probe beneath defenses and bring unconscious material into awareness. This is usually applied to "neurotic" conditions and is not advised in acute or severe schizophrenic disorders, where much of the problem is due to already weakened defenses that allow too much unconscious material to surface.

There has been a good deal of recent popular interest in the treatment of schizophrenic disorders with high doses of vitamins and trace elements. At this writing, such approaches have not really been shown to be helpful in any consistent scientific studies, but research proceeds and some people swear by the vitamin treatments. Hospitalization is often, but by no means always, necessary in the treatment of schizophrenic disorders. If the disorder is severe, hospitalization can be of great help in limiting the duration of the illness as well as decreasing the danger of suicide or homicide. While psychiatric hospitalization is generally a humiliating and degrading experience, it is often lifesaving.

Paranoid Disorders

The paranoid disorders constitute a small group of syndromes that are characterized by the same kinds of delusions and fears encountered in paranoid schizophrenia, often to greater extremes, but without the disorganization of thinking or disturbances in feeling tone seen in schizophrenia. Here, the delusions are not generally about thought-control, but are more likely to take the form of belief that one is being plotted against or persecuted by others. Delusions involving extreme and unwarranted jealousy may also be seen. Rarely, one may encounter a paranoid disorder in which the delusion is shared with another person; this is the old *folie à deux.* There are also some relatively brief *paranoid states* that can occur as reactions to the stress of radical change in environment or relationship. Treatment often consists of a combination of neuroleptics and psychotherapy, and often works quite well.

Affective Disorders

The major affective disorders are marked disturbances of mood, severe depressions, elations, or cycling between these extremes. *Bipolar affective disorder* includes alternating episodes of mania and depression or repeated episodes of mania alone. Single or recurrent episodes of depression alone are classified as *major depression* rather than bipolar disorder.

In general, mania and depression can be seen as opposite "poles" of mood. In mania, the subjective mood is inappropriately high, with excessive joviality, loquaciousness, hyperactivity, grandiosity, and often extreme religious or spiritual interest. Initially one feels unusually creative, but this creativity quickly becomes distorted and essentially nonproductive. Often, unwise business ventures are undertaken, with spending exceeding one's means. Tolerance for frustration is markedly decreased. In depression, the reverse of these characteristics is encountered. Here the mood is restricted, bitter, and self-disparaging. Thinking, speech, and physical activity are decreased severely ("psychomotor retardation"), sometimes to the point of complete cessation of movement and interaction.

Both mania and depression can be accompanied by delusions. In mania, these are usually grandiose and of a nature similar to those encountered in paranoid conditions ("I have special powers and am a chosen emissary from God.") In depression, delusions are more likely to consist of a belief that one has committed some unpardonable and earthshaking sin or that something is eating away at the insides of one's body or brain. Hallucinations are rare in mania, and when they do occur they are usually associated with grandiosity, as in hearing special guiding voices. They are more common in severe depression, where they often consist of sarcastic, condemnatory voices that berate the person and may advocate suicide.

Both mania and depression are almost invariably associated with sleep disturbances and loss of appetite and weight. In addition, depressions are often accompanied by constipation, loss of sexual interest, headaches, and a variety of other physical complaints.

The affective disorders, like the schizophrenias, tend to be severe and lasting. This differentiates them from the milder and more transient mood changes experienced by most everyone from time to time. In addition, the onset of affective disorders is often not associated with severe stress; the change in mood far exceeds any natural response to environmental change.

The differentiation between affective and schizophrenic disorders is not always easy, and research seems to be pointing out increasing similarities and overlaps between the two conditions. Delusions of thought-control are especially diagnostic of schizophrenia, however, and affective disorders are not accompanied by the disorganization of thinking seen in schizophrenia.

Major depressions are often alleviated quite dramatically by antidepressant medication, which changes serotonin and norepinephrine levels in the brain. Usually antidepressants are not helpful in schizophrenia, and may occasionally make schizophrenic symptoms worse. Lithium carbonate, a simple saltlike compound, has been proven to be especially effective in the treatment of mania, probably functioning by altering the conduction of electrical impulses along nerve cells. In many cases lithium also prevents recurrent depressive episodes, especially in people who experience alternating depression and mania. Because the affective disorders are not associated with deterioration of basic thinking/feeling integrations, they are generally less severely disabling than are chronic schizophrenic disorders.

Also included as affective disorders are two milder conditions that, while of long duration, do not go to such extremes or cause such incapacitation as do the major affective disorders. One of these is *cyclothymic disorder,* a chronic adjustment characterized by mood swings, mild depression, fatigue, pessimism, and low self-esteem alternating with expansiveness, optimism, energetic creativity, and self-aggrandizement. The other mild disorder is the old depressive neurosis, or *dysthymic disorder.* This may also be called "depressive personality" and indicates a chronically inherent proclivity to depression, a general tendency to view life from a pessimistic stance and to downgrade oneself. There may be brief periods of normal mood, but one always finds oneself returning to what seems to be a "baseline" of depression. Antidepressant medication is often less effective in these conditions; psychotherapy may be of more help. Still, there is a general feeling that antidepressants should at least be tried.

Anxiety Disorders

The anxiety disorder category, comprised of three major groups, contains many of the old "neurosis" diagnoses. The first of these is *phobias,* or prolonged unrealistic fears and avoidance behaviors. Nearly everyone has some kind of phobia, snakes, spiders, closed-in places, crowds, heights, bridges, flying, and so on. These fears and avoidances of specific things are the so-called simple phobias in contrast to the increasingly common *agoraphobia,* which is a more diffuse fear of being outside, in public, or alone. Agoraphobias may seem to "grow" out of other phobias, and can often become severely incapacitating. Antidepressant medication has been found to be helpful, especially in combination with active supportive and group efforts designed to confront fearful situations. Many agoraphobia treatment programs have been established across the United States, following models initially developed in Great Britain. A kind of in-between category is *social phobia,* which includes avoidance of certain situations because of an unrealistic fear of embarrassment or humiliation in public. Behavior therapies such as "deconditioning" have proven quite helpful with simple and social phobias. In some cases, insight-oriented psychotherapy may also be needed. But many simple phobias do not require treatment at all; the issue is simply a matter of how incapacitating the phobia is.

The second group of anxiety disorders is made up of the *anxiety states.* In these, anxiety is experienced in a more diffuse way, without any readily apparent specific cause or focus. In *general anxiety disorder* the anxiousness is felt as a persistent, continuous state that lasts for months at a time. In contrast, *panic disorder* is characterized by shorter episodes of severe anxiety interspersed with periods of freedom from symptoms. In both cases, anxiety is characterized by strong inner feelings of dread and apprehension accompanied by physical signs of anxiety such as sweating, trembling, rapid breathing and heart rate, light-headedness, and palpitations.

Also included as an anxiety state is the diagnosis *obsessive compulsive disorder.* A classic neurosis in earlier nomenclatures, this disorder is characterized by attempts to deal with anxiety through obsessions (unwanted persistent and recurrent thoughts, images, or impulses) and compulsions (unwanted persistent recurrent behaviors). Here again, nearly everyone has experienced both of these symptoms in mild degrees. Common obsessions are the song that you cannot get out of your head or the worry that keeps coming to mind and troubling you when you know there is nothing to be gained by stewing over it. Common compulsions include counting the cracks on the sidewalk or the tiles on the wall without really wanting to or having to recheck the door locks or the alarm clock before going to bed. While some obsessive compulsive behavior is "normal" and may even be helpful in ensuring attention to detail, in an obsessive compulsive disorder it is so prominent and severe that it causes great distress to the individual and significantly interferes with functioning. Classic examples of this degree of severity include extreme and protracted hand-washing, having to go through a specific number of preliminary movements before sitting down, having to retrace one's steps a certain number of times before proceeding, or having to recite some phrase or recount some series of thoughts before speaking. Severe anxiety may be experienced if one is prevented from carrying out these thoughts or behaviors.

Obsessive compulsive behaviors are characteristically ritualized, consisting of rigidly specified sequences and patterns of thought and action. As such, they are closely allied with many forms of superstition. But they should not be confused with the repetitive and ritualized patterns so characteristic of many religious practices. While worship and prayer rituals or meditative mantras can be and often are used obsessively, compulsively, or superstitiously, this is by no means their primary intent. Calling rosary beads "worry-beads" is an example of confusing prayer ritual with superstition. The difference lies in the intent behind the use. In compulsive or superstitious usage, the intent is to achieve control either of one's own anxiety or of spiritual forces. In legitimate prayerful usage, the intent is to facilitate attention and depth of awareness in prayer.

Treatment of anxiety states and obsessive compulsive disorders seems to be at its best when combining behavior-modification approaches with both supportive and insight-oriented psychotherapy and instruction in relaxation techniques. Occasionally antidepressant medication may help. Tranquilizers generally do not, and in my opinion should never be employed in these conditions. Chemical alleviation of anxiety in such disorders can easily lead to abuse or dependence, because the need to kill the distress is so great. Further, the attempt to dull oneself to anxiety contradicts the major principle of therapy for these problems, which is that the anxiety needs to be confronted.

The issue of control is especially critical to people suffering from obsessive-compulsive disorders. They may experience great panic at even the notion of surrendering control, yet they desperately long to be able to relax and allow. In spiritual direction they may have immense difficulty with spiritual surrender even in small doses, but they may also work more diligently and be more dedicated in practice than anyone else.

Somatoform Disorders

Covering many of the problems previously called neurotic, hysterical, or hypochondriacal, the category of somatoform disorders includes all bodily symptoms (pain, paralysis, strange sensations, and so on) that do not have an organic cause and can be identified as resulting from psychological factors. The *conversion reactions* such as "hysterical" blindness, paralysis, and fainting, which were so common in the Victorian era, are becoming increasingly rare in modern Western society. Presumably this has something to do with the increasing psychological sophistication of our culture. People are nowadays much less likely to believe in such symptoms and are more ready to say "It's all in your head." Thus, the secondary psychological payoff for this kind of problem is diminished, and it occurs less frequently. Instead, unconscious conflicts and impulses are more likely to become manifest as diffuse anxiety or depression.

Still, classic conversion symptoms do appear, especially in people of certain specific cultural or ethnic backgrounds. In addition, many cases of stigmata and other physical manifestations of a spiritual or religious nature have been labeled as forms of conversion or hysteria. Although this is often an accurate description, there are occasions when such a label seems to be affixed simply because there appears to be no better scientific explanation. As one psychiatric source puts it, "Divine explanations are not a basis for scientific understanding, just as scientific understanding does not nullify religious concepts. . . ."[5]

Also included as a somatoform disorder is *hypochondriasis,* a constant and severe preoccupation with the possibility of having a serious illness. Here the problem is not so much the psychological production of physical symptoms as the unrealistic fear of having a real illness.

Dissociative Disorders

Dissociative disorders are quite similar to the somatoform disorders, and also include many problems previously identified as neurotic. Here we find *psychological amnesia,* as distinguished from loss of memory due to physical causes; *fugue states,* in which one may unknowingly travel away from home and assume a new identity; and the dramatic cases of *multiple personality* in which at any given time a person is dominated by one of several distinct and apparently complete personalities. While rare, this latter state sometimes raises questions of possession by demonic or other spiritual forces and may require spiritual as well as psychiatric appraisal.[6]

In general, dissociative disorders constitute an alteration of awareness in which the individual's self-image is in one way or another divorced (dis-associated) from immediate surroundings and habitual orientations. This is clearly identifiable in *depersonalization disorder.* Here, the person experiences a feeling of unreality or radical change in self-image accompanied by an atmosphere of alien sensation—as if looking into a mirror and seeing an unfamiliar face.

Since dissociative disorders are intimately related both to self-image and to the quality or atmosphere of awareness, they constitute some of the more likely points of confusion in relation to spiritual experiences. Many experiences of dissociation occur naturally in meditation or quiet prayer. Sometimes the experience is a fully legitimate manifestation of ascetical practice or even a sign of graced spiritual growth or insight. In charismatic circles, for example, being "slain by the Spirit" or speaking in tongues—which are clearly dissociative phenomena by definition—are seen as direct manifestations or gifts of the Holy Spirit. In a purely psychiatric sense, any experience in which self-image and sensory perceptions undergo a significant change in relationship within awareness could be called dissociative. Similarly the so-called altered states of awareness so often encountered in spiritual practice would generally be considered forms of dissociation.[7]

But this label need not mean pathology. True, the psychiatric usage of "dissociation" generally implies some kind of defensive maneuver, a mechanism whereby awareness is protected from uncomfortable or unacceptable insight by being divorced from usual self-image and sensory perceptions. But if meditative experiences can be identified as explorations rather than avoidances or as natural deepenings of insight instead of defenses against insight, then the implied dissociation may reflect a more accurate perception of truth instead of a more distorted one. Further, in order to be called a disorder, a pattern of behavior must interfere with one's functioning or cause destruction to others. Since the fruits of legitimate spiritual dissociations are improved functioning and creative compassion for others, they can hardly be called disorders.

Spiritual disciplines generally assume, in fact, that our usual perceptions of self, world, and awareness are not fully accurate. They are too colored by our self-importance and our attachments, and they frequently blind us to the truth of life in God. Thus a "dissociation" that produces radically different yet more accurate perception might properly be called a "new-order" instead of a "dis-order."

One of the difficulties between psychiatry and spirituality is that psychiatry often tends to assume that "normal" or "usual" perceptions of self and world are the best, and that divergences therefrom are to be viewed with suspicion. But in religious terms what is normal in this world is most certainly not best. Instead, one looks for a *transformation* or *metanoia,* a radical and saving change in perception and being, a new birth.[8] Whether this change takes place in a single sudden conversion or through a slow process of growth, it is to be expected that it will be accompanied by some dissociative experiences. Later, when integration of the experience has occurred and one perceives something like "I am a new person in Christ," it might be said that a "re-association" has taken place at a new level of being.

But of course this is not to say that a given dissociative experience is necessarily healthy, creative, or "legitimate" just because it happens to occur within a spiritual context. History is filled with cases of individuals and groups becoming spiritually fanatical as an expression of psychological defensiveness and distortion. Many spiritual dissociations are indeed disorders in that they are defensive and interfere with functioning. Spiritual directors are often better than psychiatrists at identifying this, for discernment is needed. Does the experience seem to be really "given" to the person instead of being desperately sought after? Does it encourage a deepened willingness to meet the world more fully, or does it seem to be more of an escape from the world? Does it foster feelings of self-importance and autonomous mastery, or does it deepen humility and realization of dependence upon God? Is it appreciated for its fruits, or for its drama and excitement? Does it deepen or diminish compassion? And what is the atmosphere of awareness within which it occurs; is awareness light and loving and open; or is it dark, tense, filled with striving and drivenness, or restricted?

Both somatoform and dissociative problems must be severe enough or protracted enough to constitute a significant disturbance in personal comfort or life-functioning to be called disorders and warrant psychiatric treatment. Everyone can expect to experience transient physical symptoms or disordered perceptions in response to stress, and the vast majority of these reactions require no treatment at all. When treatment is indicated, many physicians are tempted to prescribe tranquilizers or sedatives. As in anxiety states or post-traumatic disorders, these are often of more harm than help. Insight-oriented psychotherapy is generally most advisable for these conditions, in the hope that their internal and external sources might be identified, accepted, and truly dealt with. Chemicals may temporarily alleviate the superficial symptoms, but that is all.

Psychosexual Disorders

The large category of psychosexual disorders comprises a wide variety of problems relating to sexuality. It includes *gender identity disorders* (desires to be of the opposite sex, transsexualism, and so on) and *paraphilias* (popularly known as sexual deviations and including fetishism, pedophilia, voyeurism, sadism, masochism, and so on). Also included are the *psychosexual dysfunctions* such as premature ejaculation or inhibition of desire, excitement, or orgasm. These new categories reflect a striking leap forward in the understanding of human sexual behavior, and are much more accurate, specific, and useful than old terms like "impotence" or "frigidity." Again, sexual behavior becomes a disorder when it causes distress or destruction for oneself or others. Treatment varies considerably, with many new behavioral techniques available for the psychosexual dysfunctions; group work and behavorial conditioning for the paraphilias; and supportive counseling—and even occasionally surgery—for the gender identity disorders. Of course the most common atmosphere surrounding these disorders as they apply to spiritual direction is guilt, shame, and embarrassment. As we have discussed earlier, it might be hoped that spiritual directors could at least allow for open discussion of sexuality regardless of their personal psychological and moral orientations.

Disorders of Impulse Control

This is one of several catchall categories designed to cover disorders not classifiable elsewhere. Here are mentioned pathological gambling, kleptomania, and pyromania. Also included are more recently identified *explosive disorders* in which there is either a pattern or a single episode of unpremeditated, sudden aggressive behavior that is out of character and out of proportion to the situation. Many such disorders are eventually found to be associated with some physical abnormality of the brain, and thus would fall into another category.

Adjustment Disorders

Adjustment disorders are extreme or seriously disturbing reactions to environmental stress. They may include excessive depression, anxiety, antisocial behavior, inhibition of work performance, and so on. To make this diagnosis, one must find that the response is unusual for the person, and one must feel that the disorder would disappear if the stress were removed.

Personality Disorders

The personality disorders are considered to be in a different category from the others (coded on a different "axis" in *DSM-III*). These disorders are not considered to be illnesses in the full sense of the term. More accurately, they represent character styles or personality types that are sufficiently strong and rigid to create some long-term and significant difficulty in relating to other people, in getting along with society, or in personal functioning. Further, these disorders do not come and go, but are constant features of a person's overall character. The specific labels with a few representative features are:

paranoid: suspiciousness, mistrust, hypersensitivity, coldness.
schizoid: withdrawal, introversion, insensitivity to others, lack of emotion.
schizotypal: eccentricity, magical thinking, illusions.
histrionic: dramatics, attention-seeking, vanity, seductiveness.
narcissistic: self-importance, exploitation, lack of empathy.
antisocial: frequent trouble with the law, jobs, marriages; violation of the rights of others.
borderline: impulsiveness, unstable mood, weak self-image, self-destructive behavior.
avoidant: expectation of rejection, withdrawal, negative self-image.
dependent: avoidance of responsibility, reliance on others to make decisions, difficulty being alone, toleration of much abuse from others.
compulsive: work-orientation, trouble acknowledging feelings, stinginess, indecisiveness.
passive-aggressive: stubbornness, passive resistance, intentional inefficiency.

Treatment for personality disorders generally consists of growth in self-understanding, comprehension of the effects of one's behavior, and active struggle to change habitual behaviors. Insight-oriented therapy may be helpful in some instances, and group therapy is often especially rewarding. But a concerted, self-motivated, and persistent attempt to change is required, and often this is not very strong. The life-adjustment in most personality disorders works well enough to avoid severe distress, and responsibility for change is often disowned. Both of these factors diminish motivation in many people.

It should be emphasized again that these are descriptions of personality styles that have become severe enough to constitute some kind of "problem." Everyone has a number of these characteristics, especially at times, and probably everyone could be categorized as having one of these personality styles. I, for example, tend to be compulsive. I sometimes experience ideas more than feelings, my self-image is strongly dependent upon my work performance, I am frequently anxious about spending money and would be a miser if I had my way, and it sometimes seems cosmically unfair to me that I should have to make any choices or decisions whatsoever. With most people, however, the style of personality does not create sufficient problems to warrant being called a disorder.

Labeling and Spiritual Direction

Ideally, there should be no need for extensive labeling of any kind in spiritual direction. Whether labeling assumes psychiatric or religious trappings, its overuse is likely to objectify the person and unnecessarily reduce the wonder of his or her reality. Somehow it always seems difficult to label an attribute without carrying it too far and labeling the *person*. Labeling is all too often a reductionistic process, causing us to focus on one or a few characteristics of a soul to the exclusion of others. Therefore, while it is very good to know something of how we come to be the way we are and the kinds of things that can go wrong with us, we must be vigilant not to let such knowledge get in the way of our wonder.

8. Colleagueship: Referral, Consultation, and Collaboration

The ready availability of psychiatric consultation and psychological therapies in our society is a mixed blessing. The unquestionably good side of it is that effective help for a host of difficulties is more accessible now than at any previous time in the history of the world. The bad side is that this accessibility makes it easy for referrals to be made for sinister reasons. A spiritual director can make a referral for reasons of unconscious antagonism or fear, or simply because the director wants to evade a threatening or perplexing problem. In community or institutional settings the director may succumb to administrative pressure to refer a directee. Such distorted referrals can be very damaging to the directee and should be avoided at all costs. Two examples can be given here.

The first is an early experience I had with therapy, not direction. During my psychiatric residency, I was working with a middle-aged man who was very lonely, passive, and dependent. He also was manipulative in the therapy sessions and spent most of his time in attention-seeking behaviors designed to ensure my interest in him. He would act in a coy, childish way that I found particularly distasteful. Try as I might, I was unable to "get him to see" the manipulative qualities of his behavior. It seemed all he wanted to do was bask in the pleasure of talking to me. After he started calling me during off-hours I began to feel that I just could not deal with him. My supervisor suggested I put him in a group that I was leading, but I had other, unconsciously determined, plans in mind.

In one of the many sessions during which we discussed his use or misuse of therapy, I said, "I think you would benefit more from psychoanalysis." I subsequently referred him to a local analyst. Although I really believed this was best at the time, I later realized that I had in actuality been trying to get him out of my life entirely. The man seemed pleased and happy that I considered his problems serious enough to warrant psychoanalysis. The analyst, however, was not. After reviewing the situation, the analyst informed me that this man was one of the least suited for analysis that he had ever met.

I did a little personal therapy about this, identified my own fear of responsibility and my repugnance against such excessive dependency, and wound up with the man in a group as my supervisor had initially suggested. The group helped confront him with his behavior, and he began to make some progress. Although things worked out, my own need to refer this person had not helped him because it was not dealt with directly. It would have been much better to have been honest with him, whether I actually wound up referring him or not.

In another example, a male spiritual director referred a male directee for psychiatric treatment after almost two years of spiritual direction. The referral came as a total surprise to the directee. All the director said was "I think you may have some issues that you need to deal with that we can't handle in direction. You need therapy to supplement direction." When the directee asked what these issues were, the director said he did not want to discuss them because it might interfere with the proposed therapy.

After a while, the directee was able to convince the director that his request made no sense. "I'd be glad to consider therapy," he said, "but let's say I do go see a therapist. What am I supposed to say? I can't just say 'my spiritual director thought it would be a good idea.' I do trust your judgment, but frankly there's something fishy going on here."

The director first confided that he suspected the directee had some sexual problems, and finally admitted that he, the director, had been quite distressed when in an earlier session the directee had reported a sexual fantasy involving Jesus. He felt that "it just couldn't be normal," even though the directee had affirmed that it was just a fantasy and only a transient way in which his mind was attempting to comprehend the incomprehensible love expressed in Jesus.

Here too the relationship was salvaged. The director embarked on a more concerted exploration of his own sexuality, and found himself very grateful for what the directee had pointed out to him. In a later meeting the director said "You know, if anybody needed therapy, it was me. But really I guess neither of us did. I can see that I have some sexual hang-ups just like everyone else, and I feel more confident that they won't interfere with my perceptions so much in the future. The real problem was that I got so hooked by one of your experiences that I lost sight of your overall growth in God. I know that sounds familiar, because I'm always telling you not to take any special experience too seriously. I guess I need to practice what I preach. Anyway, I think it was a graced moment for both of us. You saw some of my fallibility and I was reminded of what is really important and what isn't."

The Dynamics of Referral

It is obvious that any consideration of psychiatric referral must be carefully examined by the director. Is there any sense of personal confusion on the part of the director? Are the reasons especially vague or unclear? Does the idea of referral come up suddenly and surprisingly in a relationship that otherwise seems to have been going well? And perhaps most importantly, is the director reluctant to share his or her reasons for the recommendation?

In addition, the possibility of referral must be discussed mutually so that a joint decision can be made. If counseling or psychotherapy is really going to be of help, the individual must recognize the need and have some personal motivation. There are rare exceptions to this rule, as in some cases of child abuse or antisocial behavior in which the courts, the family, or other parties are sufficiently involved to "create" motivation within a person. Otherwise, the desire and motivation must be fully owned by the individual for therapy to be effective.

There must also be an honest appraisal of the connection between the referral and the direction relationship. Does the idea of referral arise as a way of dealing with discomfort in the relationship? Is one thinking of "getting rid" of a directee in this way, or is it assumed that direction will continue along with therapy? How is the notion of referral going to affect the relationship? Will the directee see it as a rejection or a devaluing of his or her personal competence? Could it in fact be such a rejection? How is the referral likely to affect the openness of awareness during subsequent meetings? Will it stimulate a "problem-solving" mentality that will interfere with attention to grace, or will it relieve the direction relationship from problem preoccupations and enable greater openness? Can it really be a mutual decision, or will it aggravate problems of authority and submission? Not all of these questions can be answered in advance, of course, but they should at least be recognized and given some ongoing attention.

Finally, the decision about referral should be a matter of discernment rather than objective diagnosis. In private and mutual prayer and reflection, the idea of referral should come to be associated with a sense of graced potential, a feeling of "rightness" as compared to a frantic and driven need to accomplish something. Even in situations of psychological crisis there is time for at least some prayerful attention and calling upon the Lord for guidance.

Indications for Referral

As mentioned earlier, sometimes people will come for spiritual direction when what they really need is therapy. It should become obvious within the first few sessions whether a person is primarily interested in deepening realization or in solving psychological problems. If therapy is needed, one should make a referral, but it is also necessary to discern whether direction should be initiated concurrently with therapy. In most such cases it is probably better to evalute this after therapy has had a chance to improve the person's perspective. Thus one might say "Let's see how the therapy goes and plan to meet again in six months or so to consider spiritual direction." Occasionally however, spiritual and psychodynamic issues are so intertwined that a person needs to begin direction and therapy simultaneously.

In the course of spiritual direction that is well under way, the situations in which psychiatric or psychological referral is called for can be grouped into two general categories, those that must take place of necessity, and those that can be helpful on the basis of expediency. The finest distinctions between these two groups are not always clear. There are some people who would feel that psychological assistance is never absolutely necessary, that one can make it through any conceivable situation with faith, grace, and one's own resources. At the other extreme are adherents to the more modern assumption that spiritual growth is impossible without a hefty psychological self-exploration, and that any emotional distress is cause for therapy. Since neither of these extremes makes too much real sense, we are bound to walk a middle ground in which necessity and expediency are often uncertain. While we may not always be able to tell the difference, it can be helpful to know that a difference exists.

Necessary Referrals

In actuality, truly necessary referrals are quite few. They involve situations of imminent danger to life, limb, or property. Most obviously here, one thinks of homicide and suicide. While it is very uncommon for people in spiritual direction to actually commit either act (they generally have too much existential freedom to feel so trapped), it can happen, and it will become more frequent as a larger percentage of the population seeks spiritual direction. It can happen in connection with any number of the above-mentioned psychiatric disorders, most notably in depression, mania, or schizophrenia, or in rare instances it may occur in a person who is not obviously "diagnosable."[1]

It is a well-established fact that most people who commit suicide have given clues as to their upcoming act, and although clues are less frequent and clear with homicide, these, too, often exist. The most obvious of these are signs of depression and rage, feelings of powerlessness and hopelessness, prior self-destructive or violent behavior, and of course, threats.

It is another well-established fact that the best way to find out whether a person is contemplating such an act is to *ask*. The old myth of avoiding such topics for fear of putting the idea into someone's head has been pretty much discredited. It still may take a little extra courage to come out and ask a depressed person about suicidal thoughts or an enraged person about murderous or aggressive impulses, but since such questions can be lifesaving, the discomfort is worth it.

Sometimes it is easier to move up to the topic gradually. If a person can be encouraged to talk about feelings of depression, then it becomes quite natural to ask "Have you been feeling that life isn't worth it, or that you'd be better off dead?" If the answer is yes, one follows it with "Have you had some thoughts about taking your life or hurting yourself?" If a person is really depressed, there probably have been some thoughts about suicide. It would be very unusual if there had not been. Thus if someone maintains that such a thought has never crossed his or her mind, one must have a little doubt about the honesty of the response.

If thoughts about suicide are admitted, it is important to distinguish whether they are simply transient, fleeting ideas that are not given serious consideration or ideas being seriously entertained. Are such thoughts frightening? (usually a good sign) or comforting and seductive? (usually a bad sign). Then, one must proceed to ask if any plans exist. Has the person actually been thinking about how to do it? Are the means of accomplishing it available? Finally, does the person really intend to do it?

The serious entertaining of suicidal thoughts is in my opinion sufficient cause for a necessary psychiatric referral, at least for consultation. It may turn out that thinking suicidal thoughts is a relatively innocuous habit, but one never knows. From here on, the immediacy of the danger increases dramatically. "Making plans" means one had better not wait long for the consultation. "Actual intent with available means" constitutes an emergency requiring immediately getting the person to a hospital or to a physician who can admit to a hospital. The best immediate source of help in such instances is the nearest hospital emergency room, and family members can be enlisted to aid in getting the person there. It is, of course, always wise to try to talk the person out of suicide, but never rely on this alone.

If, and only if, the relationship is solid and trusting, some time can be bought by committing the person to an agreement that no action will be taken until there has been a chance to work out some consultation or referral arrangements, or by extracting a *willing* promise to call you before doing anything. But if you do not feel comfortable with such an arrangement, don't trust it.

A similar series of questions can often reveal homicidal or assaultive intent. Again, one can begin gradually: "I guess you get pretty angry about this?" "Do you sometimes feel like getting back at him?" "How might you do it?" Ever feel like killing him?" "Have you seriously considered it?" "Do you think you really might?" "What do you think the chances are?" Any serious consideration of violence or history of past physical attacks constitute necessity for referral, and the immediacy of the need increases with each affirmative response thereafter.

It is especially important to remember that the likelihood of suicide, homicide, aggressive outbursts, and other destructive behavior is dramatically increased if alcohol is part of the picture. Alcohol lowers natural behavioral inhibitions, encourages impulsivity, and impairs what little good judgment may be left in a disturbed mind. In some people, the direct chemical effects of alcohol can trigger violence in the absence of any other precipitating factors.

The second situation in which referral can be considered a necessity is when the behavior associated with a mental disorder threatens to ruin one's life-situation or relationships to such a degree that irrevocable and unhealable wounds are left. This is much more a matter of personal judgment, and opinions may vary considerably as to how much one can really lose professionally or socially without suffering irreparable damage. For some, it might seem a necessity to prevent the loss of a job from depressive or schizophrenic incapacitation; the squandering of assets in mania; or the destruction of family or social relationships as a result of paranoia or alcoholism. For others, the prevention of such losses might seem more expedient than necessary. But it must be remembered that these kinds of losses are not simply financial and social. They can leave serious psychological and even spiritual wounds. As but one example, people with bipolar affective disorders can be thrust into ever-deepening depression with the realization of how much they have lost and squandered during manic episodes.

The third condition of necessity for referral is treatable organic illness. Any mental disorder accompanied by physical symptoms is an occasion for psychiatric referral, as is any evidence of organic mental disorder (signs of impaired memory, orientation, attention, or the like that might signal dementia, delirium, or other organic brain problems). Some of these conditions can be life-threatening, and may masquerade as purely psychological phenomena.

Upon the occasion of *any* significant physical symptom or of any psychological symptom that is not immediately and obviously identifiable, one should at least encourage the directee to have a thorough physical examination. Even if specialized psychiatric consultation is not needed, a general physical often is. Thyroid problems, for example, can appear as anxiety disorder, depression, or mania. Tumors of the adrenal gland can produce many of the symptoms of schizophrenia, paranoia, or major depressive disorder. A host of other physical problems can appear in the guise of psychological symptoms.

This emphasizes the danger of trying to "make" diagnoses, and also raises the idea that spiritual directors might take some responsibility for ensuring that their directees take care of their physical health. It would certainly be wise not only to encourage medical evaluation for any symptoms, but also to make sure that regular physical examinations are sought by the directee. This is certainly in keeping with the director's role of attention to the whole person, and need not interfere with attentiveness to more precisely "spiritual" matters.

Expedient Referrals

One obvious expedient referral occurs when a mental disorder threatens to disrupt a person's life-situation in a needless way. This is, of course, a matter of judgment, but it can be advised that any persistent or severe pattern of maladjustment that is liable to affect the directee's life in any destructive way is worthy of discussing with a view to referral.

In a similar vein, conditions that cause needless suffering to the individual, and for which there is some possibility of treatment, should be discussed. For example, it could be very rewarding to discuss an anxiety disorder that keeps a person constantly ill at ease, even though it does not really interfere with functioning.

What existential significance does this disorder have to the directee? How does it relate to or affect prayer life? Why has professional help not been sought previously? What does this say about
the person's attitude towards self, God, and suffering? Might there
be some unrealistic sense of *needing* to suffer? Or is the acceptance
of the condition a legitimate spiritual surrender of oneself to the
care of the divine?

This kind of surrender and acceptance can be very legitimate,
especially if the disorder is not harmful to one's functioning or
interactions with others. But more often there are covert reasons
for failing to seek help. Perhaps one thinks some special merit is to
be gained by suffering needlessly. Perhaps there is some kind of
"martyr" complex unconsciously designed to instill guilt in others.
Or there may be an underlying depression that eradicates hope and
encourages self-punishment. There may be some prideful shame
and embarrassment surrounding the need for psychological help.
Or maybe the person is actually convinced that there is something
fundamentally wrong with feeling good. Discussion of such matters
can take place without disrupting the atmosphere of spiritual direction if they are acknowledged as intimately related to the interaction of self-image with grace and of self—will with divine will.

Referral might also be considered when an individual's preoccupation with personal or relational problems is so severe that it fills
spiritual direction sessions and eclipses prayerful attention to the
divine. This kind of preoccupation is to be expected in everyone
during transient times of crisis—and may even be an opportunity
to look for God's calling in the midst of the distraction—but if it
begins to form a pattern, spiritual direction may be impossible until some perspective is gained on the problem. If this perspective
cannot be attained in direction, consultation or referral is called
for.

Sometimes psychological or relational difficulties are so severe
that they demand the person's attention and thus forcibly prevent a
larger, deeper spiritual attentiveness. At other times, psychological
difficulties make a person so self-concerned and self—preoccupied
that he or she is consistently blinded to spiritual insight. And at
still other times, one may consciously or unconsciously use psychological problems to avoid spiritual insight. All of these possibilities

may need discussion in spiritual direction, and some of them may be greatly helped by referral.

There are also occasions in which inner psychodynamics or old "baggage" actually constitute blocks to spiritual progress. One woman was stymied in her spiritual practice until she could deal with old and powerful feelings about her masculine image of God. One man was so threatened by the experience of relaxing and its associated threat of losing control that he could hardly pray. Situations like this usually can and should be handled within the direction situation itself without any need for referral. But if it does prove necessary, referral should not be avoided.

In addition, it is neither always necessary nor advisable to work all such problems through to their final psychological resolution. Many of them can be legitimately circumvented. For example, the woman who was blocked by her male God-image identified a few of her feelings about men and freed a bit of her anger about being a woman in our society, but most importantly she was able to experience that her image of God was *not God*. Her prayer opened up when she discovered how to move *through* that image into a deeper appreciation of the divine mystery behind all images. She had certainly not resolved all her feelings, but her stumbling block in prayer had been bypassed. She was free to continue to deal with her other feelings in the course of her life and prayer.

Upon recognizing a psychological problem in ourselves or in someone else, we often make the mistake of assuming that it must be worked through and resolved before progress in the spiritual life is possible. This is simply—and fortunately—not true. As Freud pointed out in his *Psychopathology of Everyday Life* and *Analysis Terminable and Interminable,* our minds can be literally endless reservoirs of things that appear to need working through. It is a great waste of time to lose oneself in personal psychology in order to prepare oneself for a better life, for such endeavors can easily take place at the expense of life, and they can go on forever. Further, such self-preoccupation tends to deny the potential for God's graced, active intervention in our spiritual searching and encourages us to assume that we both need to and are able to perfect ourselves.

While psychological blocks to spiritual growth certainly do occur, most can be handled in spiritual direction settings—and should be. Only a few of the most stubborn of these will require psychiatric or psychological referral. The director and directee need to reflect first on whether a psychological problem is actually interfering with spiritual awareness or practice. If it is, can it be "cut through" or circumvented legitimately or must time and energy be taken to deal with it? And if this time and energy are necessary, would it be best to use spiritual direction time or to set up concurrent therapy arrangements?

Finally, an expedient psychiatric consultation may be made in those rare situations in which one simply cannot discern whether some protracted experience is a condition of spiritual growth or a manifestation of psychological disorder. At such times, discernment and diagnosis can function quite complementarily. For example, one might feel stymied as to whether a protracted emptiness or aridity in prayer as a result of depression, a "dark-night" realization, or some combination of the two. If the aridity goes on without clarification, psychiatric consultation might do a lot to help gain a perspective on the situation. While one would not generally expect a psychiatrist to discern the "dark night," he or she could be very helpful in identifying depressive symptoms or predispositions, and could contribute very useful information. Such consultation may be helpful for any situation that remains confusing in spiritual direction.

The Mechanism of Referral

As indicated, all considerations of consultation or referral should be made jointly and be part of an overall discernment process, except in exceedingly rare emergency situations. Some people have trouble raising the idea of psychiatric assistance for fear it will be taken as an insult. In such instances it is probably better to present the possibility in a forthright manner, taking the risk rather than "beating around the bush." Psychiatric consultations and therapy are, after all, legitimate options in this day and age, and it serves no purpose to support old embarrassments about the possibility.

One thing that should be dealt with carefully, however, is the effect the referral discussion may have on the directee's feelings about the direction relationship. The directee may experience some uneasiness in terms of self-confidence or even confidence in the director. This is especially likely if dependency or transference has become an issue. There may be a sense that "my situation is too much for him to handle," or "maybe she thinks I'm cracking up." Thus, during or after the discussion of the actual issues surrounding the possibility of referral, the director should always ask for any other feelings, doubts, or uneasiness in response to the discussion.

A decision needs to be made as to whether the director will recommend a specific psychiatrist or psychologist for the referral, or whether this will be left up to the directee. Similarly, there is the possibility of the director actually making the initial contact for the directee. Usually the directee can express his or her desires along these lines quite clearly. In some cases, the director may want to stay out of the picture as much as possible, to avoid blurring the distinction between caring *for* the person's soul and taking care *of* of the person's life. At other times it may be expedient or helpful for the director to play a more active part. This is especially true in cases of consultation concerning discernment or relationship confusions.

In any case, special attention has to be paid to the confidentiality of the relationship. Only at the express request of the directee should the director discuss his or her situation with a third party. Ideally, the directee should be present when any discussions between psychiatrist and director take place. This may not always be possible, but the implications of two people "discussing me behind my back" are so loaded—even when there is substantial trust— that every attempt should be made to involve all three parties in the interchange.

If the director does have some contact with the psychiatrist at the beginning, or is likely to meet the psychiatrist from time to time, it should be clearly understood whether there will be any discussion of the directee. Even the slightest references such as "How are things going with Joe?" or "Are you still seeing Judy?" can create insoluble confidentiality problems for everyone if there has been no clear agreement ahead of time.

It is becoming increasingly common for a person to be in psychotherapy and spiritual direction at the same time. This may happen because the therapist suggested direction, or the director suggested therapy, or the individual simply saw the need for both. In most cases this can constitute a very comfortable and helpful arrangement. The director can be more free to keep the focus on spiritual issues, knowing that there is an ongoing opportunity for dealing with psychodynamics, and the directee can be clear about what to bring up where. In fact, some directors do not fully understand the difference between spiritual direction and psychotherapy until they have worked with someone who is in both.

But all is not necessarily perfect in such arrangements. Directors may avoid dealing with psychodynamic issues that impinge upon the directee's prayer life, either because of an unrealistic fear of treading on the therapist's "territory" or because such avoidance is an easy "cop-out." If the nature and purpose of spiritual direction are not clearly understood by the directee, he or she may confuse the two. This can usually be handled by some direct clarification and ground rules about what the focus is to be in both undertakings. But occasionally a directee may use direction to avoid dealing with something uncomfortable in therapy, or may "act out" some transference issues from therapy in the direction relationship. This can get to be sticky, and if direct examination of the behavior is unrewarding, a three-way meeting may be needed to get things moving again.

Colleagueship

It is evident from the above discussions that spiritual directors would do well to have established some resource connections within the behavioral science community. It is worth checking around for such contacts before the need arises, and one will discover that making the acquaintance of psychologists, psychiatrists, and other professionals can prove personally rewarding as well as vocationally expedient. They may call you for consultation on spiritual matters, and you may call them for help with psychological issues. When this kind of colleagueship can be established, one gains a very reassuring sense of the larger community of help that is available for everyone.

There is in my opinion nothing wrong with a quick call to a colleague about a special problem encountered in spiritual direction, just as it makes sense for a psychiatrist to call regarding a spiritual issue with which a patient is struggling. But the most absolute care must be taken to ensure—not protect, but ensure—the anonymity of the directee or patient. If there is any doubt whatsoever about this, as for example, the remote possibility that the psychiatrist might know the person in another setting, then one had best not even broach the topic without the directee's express permission and request. Most often, a situation or an experience can be described hypothetically without giving any identifiable description of the person involved. But the importance of confidentiality is so crucial that it cannot be overemphasized. There is little that can destroy a relationship and wound the spirit more than a breach of confidence.

In establishing resource connections and considering consultation or referral, it should be remembered that psychiatrists are physicians who can address physical problems and prescribe medication while psychologists are usually less skilled in the medical arts and more adept at psychological testing. Social workers may be more competent at family interventions. Thus, for a diagnostic question involving the possibility of physical illness, or when major mental illness is likely, psychiatric consultation is advised. But when it comes to psychotherapy, the personal orientation and character of the therapist are far more important than his or her professional title. Many psychologists are more gifted and skilled as therapists than are many psychiatrists. Some social workers also do insight-oriented therapy, but most are better trained in offering supportive care. Pastoral counselors are also generally trained in supportive therapies, especially of the humanistic school.

When one needs to consider referral for certain special problems, it is good to know that programs designed especially for certain disorders may be more helpful than general psychiatric or psychological services. For example, alcoholism and other chemical abuses and dependencies are better handled through A.A. and specific drug and alcohol treatment programs than through individual therapy. And as mentioned before, specific centers have been set up for the treatment of phobias. Similar programs exist that are designed to deal with sexual dysfunction, sleep disorders, and violence. There are also special programs for identified populations such as adolescents, abused wives, and senior citizens. The best way to identify useful programs and referral sources is to establish a colleagueship with one or two mental health professionals whom you can trust, and to ask their opinions.

In seeking such colleagueship it would of course be helpful to find someone who has an appreciation of and sensitivity to spiritual matters. But one needs to be careful in this regard. It is not safe to assume, for example, that a psychiatrist is really respectful of people's spiritual journeys simply because he or she is interested in "transpersonal" therapies or uses meditation or other consciousness-altering techniques. In many cases, such individuals are doing nothing more than appropriating certain spiritual techniques to achieve psychological ends. In a sense, though the person may be able to talk in spiritual jargon, this may constitute a deep *dis*respect for spirituality. Similarly, one cannot assume that the specific training of pastoral counselors or Jungian analysts conveys any inherent spiritual sensitivity. The individual's personal spirituality is what counts.

Beware of professionals who use spiritual or ascetical practices as "adjuncts" to therapy; trust more those who have a serious personal spiritual life and who use traditional, even stodgy, therapeutic methods in their vocation of helping others. It is better to deal with a psychiatrist who knows psychiatry and is willing to leave the spirit alone than one who meddles psychologically with spiritual matters.

Further, in your relationships with mental health professionals, beware of that old "almighty doctor" image. Too many people are so impressed by their own psychological ignorance in the face of professional expertise that they relinquish their own common sense. Spiritual directors may take psychiatric conclusions as gospel without understanding them, or be afraid of expressing their own opinions to a directee who is also seeing a psychiatrist. Such reactions are never helpful and often harmful. Not only must you claim your own authority in spiritual matters, but you must also claim your common sense in everything "else."

When a psychiatrist offers a diagnosis or makes a recommendation, it should make sense to you. If it does not, the psychiatrist should be able to explain it in a way that is really understandable. In other words, you should be able to agree with the conclusion based on your thinking as supplemented by the psychiatric information. Sometimes it is all too easy to defer one's own responsibilities for making judgments by simply letting the professional handle things. This is especially true in sticky interpersonal situations or when one has been plagued by confusion about some issue. But to give up one's own role like this is neither wise nor fair. In true colleagueship both parties "own" their own capabilities and responsibilities, relying on each other's knowledge, insight, and opinions to come to a mutually understandable and responsible conclusion.

I do not think this is an overly idealistic statement for the present day. There were times in the past when psychiatrists felt that religious people did nothing but go around creating psychological problems and instilling guilt in others. Then there came a time when many religious people sold out to psychiatry, adopting its anthropocentric orientation and sacrificing their own theological sensibilities in the hope of becoming "relevant" and gaining "credibility." More recently, there have been more frequent experiences in which the professions have been able to collaborate in an atmosphere of true teamwork and mutuality. But this can never happen unless both parties respect and value their own disciplines as well as each other's. Now, more than ever, with spiritual direction's increasing popularity, we are called to be the best kind of colleagues we can become.

In addition to colleagueship between spiritual directors and mental health professionals, it is exceedingly rewarding if spiritual directors can be colleagues to one another. The Shalem Institute for Spiritual Formation with which I work has found exceptional value in the establishment of "colleague groups" for spiritual directors within the Baltimore-Washington area.[2] These groups are comprised of from six to ten spiritual directors who meet regularly to discuss concerns and issues that arise in their work. They present situations occurring in direction, (with careful preservation of confidentiality) and share insights, opinions, and observations. The meetings are structured to provide time for mutual support, prayer, and questioning together. The discussions are focused not on solving the directees' problems but on the directors' own feelings, attitudes, insights, and awareness, and on the relationship of happenings in direction to the director's own spiritual life.

These groups are now coming to include increasing numbers of therapists and counselors who have discovered a calling to respond more than superficially to the spiritual needs of their patients and clients. Some, like myself, find themselves offering both spiritual direction and psychotherapy as quite distinct disciplines. We all need each other in these enterprises. At the risk of a play on words, spiritual directors need psychiatric help. And psychiatrists are in heart-deep if not always heart-felt need of spiritual help. And those of us who attempt to walk both paths need all the help we can get.

We have here an opportunity for realizing our interdependence in God, a chance for a more accurate vision than ever before of our rich, graced togetherness as incarnate members of the corporate body of Christ. My hope is that we might truly make the most of one another in the ministry of caring for the minds and spirits of our sisters and brothers.

Notes

(Full publication information is given in the Bibliography for books referred to in the Notes by the author's last name.)

CHAPTER 1
1. Leech does an admirable job in Chapter 2 of *Soul Friend.*
2. An ecumenical conference on spiritual direction, in Denver, cosponsored by Shalem and The Association of Theological Schools in the United States and Canada.
3. Buber and McNamara point out the essential humanism of Jung.
4. Leech, pp. 130–31, Edwards, pp. 57–61.
5. Edwards, pp. 61–63 and *passim,* and my *Pilgrimage Home.*
6. McNamara's term.
7. Edwards has condensed some of these ideas into a table in *Spiritual Friend,* pp. 129–32.

CHAPTER 2
1. Fowler and Whitehead have excellent descriptions. See also the Appendix of my *Open Way.*
2. Fairchild.
3. *Scientific American.*
4. Ram Dass, in *Be Here Now,* gives a fine anecdotal account of his psychedelic experiences.

CHAPTER 3
1. Fromm.
2. Rodewyk.
3. Acts 5:38–39.
4. Leech, Setzer, Futrell, Guillet, Kelsey, Rodewyk, Ignatius.
5. Jung, *The Meaning of Psychology for Modern Man,* 1934.
6. See Kelsey's *Dreams,* for example.
7. J. Allen Hobson and Robert W. McCarley, "The Brain as a Dream State Generator: An Activation-Synthesis Hypothesis of the Dream Process," *American Journal of Psychiatry* 134, no. 12 (December 1977). 1335–48.
8. This statement is based on psychodynamic theory. I have not seen such decompensations happen, but then I have also tried to avoid creating conditions in which they *might* happen.
9. Castaneda and Tulku.

CHAPTER 4
1. As in the parable of the seed or "many are called but few are chosen."
2. *Childhood and Society,* p. 247 ff.

3. *Individualization* (becoming a defined individual) is different from Carl Jung's and Otto Rank's concepts of *individuation,* which refers to becoming all one can be or is meant to be.
4. As in Acts 17:24–28.
5. See Freud's 1931 paper "Libidinal Types," in *Collected Papers.*
6. Attachment is the spiritual term that most closely corresponds to the psychoanalytic *cathexis.* Attachment involves the investment of energy in some object or cause, and it always relates to self-image.
7. It is a standard psychological maxim that people regress to earlier levels of coping when under stress. Thus it is to be expected that our childhood prayers and images of God return to us in crisis. I do not see this as at all pathological. In fact, it seems quite beautiful.

CHAPTER 5
1. See Brenner for an overview.
2. See Ignatius and Teresa of Avila for primary sources and Squire for a variety of perspectives from other classical "masters."
3. "Attempts to remedy depression" refers to such approaches as encouraging activity or seeking underlying anger. It does not include the use of any chemical agents.
4. See John of the Cross, Ignatius, Leech and Squire. My conceptions differ from the classics at several points.
5. John of the Cross gives the classic description in his *Dark Night of the Soul.* The last three chapters of Squire and Chapter 4 of Leech are especially helpful as well.

CHAPTER 6
1. Parataxic distortion was first delineated by Harry Stack Sullivan.
2. My use of the term "sexual" here refers to its limited *erotic* meaning, not the more general meanings of creative energy or radical incompleteness.
3. It must be emphasized here that repression and other defense mechanisms are not inherently bad. We could not function without them. They create problems only when they occur in excess or are unduly restrictive.
4. The etymology is interesting here. The Middle English and Anglo-Saxon words for *holy* meant "whole" or "complete." But the old Latin, Greek, *and Hebrew* words meant "set apart."

CHAPTER 7
1. McNamara describes this problem very clearly.
2. Some attempts have been made. Hora is a fine example, and Peck takes a few steps in this direction. *Transpersonal Psychology* (see the McNamara reference) dabbles in the area. My *Will and Spirit: A Contemplative Psychology* (forthcoming) also takes a stab at it.
3. Two versions of this publication are noted in the Bibliography.
4. For example, is there evidence of obstinacy rather than docility, exaggeration rather than discretion, pride rather than humility, disquiet rather than peace, duplicity rather than simplicity? These are taken from J. B. Scaramelli's list, quoted in Leech, p. 129. See other references on discernment, as well.

5. Reported in *Clinical Psychiatry News,* March 1981, p. 28. This observation was made in reference to a case of stigmatic bleeding in a young Mexican-American woman in San Antonio. The case, which was unusually well studied, defied scientific explanation. Direct examination revealed the extrusion of actual blood through intact skin with no tissue abnormalities. Stigmata were also reported in the woman's infant daughter. The case was reported by J. Fisher and E. Kollar in the *Southern Medical Journal* 73 (1980): 1461–66.

6. See the fascinating case report by J. Stevenson *et al.,* "A Case of Secondary Personality with Xenoglossy," *American Journal of Psychiatry* 136, no. 12 (December 1979).

7. See Tart's introduction to McNamara.

8. See Gratton.

CHAPTER 8

1. These include the so-called justifiable homicides and rational suicides. The moral and spiritual implications of such acts are too extensive to discuss here, but it should at least be understood that such acts are not always evidence of mental disorder. See Szasz's writings on this.

2. Edwards gives some descriptions of these, along with other programs, p. 198 and *passim.*

Bibliography

American Psychiatric Association. *Diagnostic and Statistical Manual of Mental Disorders: Third Edition.* Washington, D.C.: American Psychiatric Association, 1980. (*DSM-III.*) The full volume is rather extensive, but an abbreviated version is also available from the A.P.A. Also forthcoming are case study examples relating to *DSM-III* categories.

Assagioli, R. *Psychosynthesis.* New York: Hobbs, Dorman, 1965. A coherent attempt to integrate spiritual and psychological models and a classic in its field.

Barnhouse, R. "Spiritual Direction and Psychotherapy." *Journal of Pastoral Care* 33, no. 3 (Sept. 1979). More comparisons than contrasts between therapy and an Ignatian orientation towards spiritual direction, by a prominent Jungian analyst.

Barry, W. A. "Spiritual Direction and Pastoral Counseling." *Pastoral Psychology* 26 (Fall 1977). More comparisons and similarities.

Brenner, C. *An Elementary Textbook of Psychoanalysis.* New York: Doubleday Anchor, 1974. An excellent, concise description of Freudian theories of personality development, psychic functioning and defense mechanisms.

Buber, M. *Eclipse of God.* New York: Harper Torch Books, 1952. A "Critique of Twentieth Century Philosophies," which points out their tendencies to cloud the transcendence of God. Especially relevant is his "Reply to C. G. Jung."

Castaneda, C. *The Eagle's Gift.* New York: Simon & Schuster, 1981. Gives a radical and world-view-shaking approach to work with dreaming.

The Cloud of Unknowing and *The Book of Privy Counseling.* Edited by William Johnston. New York: Doubleday Image, 1973. A classic by an anonymous Christian mystic.

Doran, R. "Jungian Psychology and Christian Spirituality." *Review for Religious,* July, August, and September 1979. Comparisons and contrasts.

Edwards, T. *Spiritual Friend.* New York: Paulist, 1980. Excellent practical overview of contemporary Christian spiritual direction. With Leech, recommended as a general introduction.

Erikson, E. *Childhood and Society.* 2nd ed. New York: W. W. Norton, 1964. A psychological classic much used in pastoral work.

Fairchild, R. *Finding Hope Again.* San Francisco: Harper & Row, 1980. A pastoral approach to depression, including its spiritual implications.

Fowler, J. *Stages of Faith.* San Francisco: Harper & Row, 1981. Excellent example of Fowler's contemporary and strongly psychologically-oriented work on faith development.

Freud, S. "The Future of an Illusion," "Totem and Taboo," "Moses and Monotheism," "Libidinal Types," "On Narcissism." Classics relating to Freud's narrow and biased views of religion. "Libidinal Types" and "On Narcissism" give some helpful insights into self-image makeup.

Fromm, E. *The Art of Loving.* New York: Harper & Row, 1956. Another contemporary psychological classic.

Futrell, J. "Ignatian Discernment." *Studies in the Spirituality of Jesuits* 2, no. 2 (April, 1970). Self-explanatory title.

Geromel, E. "Depth Therapy and Spiritual Direction," *Review for Religious* 36 (1977). More emphasis on similarities than on distinctions.

Goldberg, M. *A Guide to Psychiatric Diagnosis and Understanding for the Helping Professions.* Chicago: Nelson-Hall, 1973. Now a little outdated diagnostically, but includes excellent practical insights. One of the best books of its kind.

Gratton, C. *Guidelines for Spiritual Direction.* Denville, New Jersey: Dimension Books, 1980. A fine little book written by a psychologist associated with Adrian van Kaam's work at Duquesne.

Guillet, J. et al. *Discernment of Spirits.* Collegeville, Minn.: Liturgical Press, 1970. Some classic approaches.

Hora, T. *Existential Metapsychiatry.* New York: Seabury, 1977. Excellent conceptual integration of Christian spirituality and contemporary psychiatry. Highly recommended.

Ignatius Loyola. *The Spiritual Exercises.* Translated by Anthony Mottola. New York: Image, 1958. Probably the most well known classic relating to discernment.

James, W. *The Varieties of Religious Experience.* New York: Modern Library, 1936. This nineteenth century classic is included because no bibliography on these matters could exclude it.

John of the Cross. *The Ascent of Mount Carmel* and *Dark Night of the*

Soul. A number of translations and editions are available. Classics of Christian mysticism.

Jung, C. G. *Memories, Dreams, and Reflections. The Meaning of Psychology for Modern Man. Modern Man in Search of a Soul. The Undiscovered Self. Psychology and Religion, West and East.* Available in a number of editions. The undisputed giant of psychospiritual considerations in spite of his inveterate humanism and inability to portray the transcendence of God.

Kelsey, M. *Dreams: A Way to Listen to God.* New York: Paulist, 1978. *Discernment: A Study in Ecstasy and Evil.* New York: Paulist, 1978. Strong Jungian emphasis with considerable contemporary relevance.

Leech, K. *Soul Friend.* San Francisco: Harper & Row, 1980. Excellent overview of Christian spiritual direction in historical cultural contexts. Recommended as a general introduction in combination with Edwards.

McNamara, W. "Psychology and the Christian Mystical Tradition." In *Transpersonal Psychologies,* edited by Charles Tart. New York: Harper & Row, 1975. In my opinion this is one of the finest pieces making *distinctions* between the disciplines. Deals with some of Jung's problems.

May, G. *Simply Sane.* New York: Paulist, 1977. A portrayal of spiritual attitudes towards growth and healing. *The Open Way.* New York: Paulist, 1977. A meditation handbook. *Pilgrimage Home.* New York: Paulist, 1979. A study of group spiritual guidance. *Will and Spirit.* San Francisco: Harper & Row, forthcoming. A contemplative psychology.

Otto, R. *The Idea of the Holy.* New York: Oxford, 1950. Another modern classic dealing with the human response to God's mystery.

Peck, M. S. *The Road Less Traveled.* New York: Simon & Schuster, 1979. A noncontemplative but very rich modern integration of concepts concerning mental health, spiritual growth, and love.

Progoff, I. *At a Journal Workshop.* New York: Dialogue House Library, 1975. The Granddaddy of journaling methodologies.

Ram Dass. *Be Here Now.* New York: Crown, 1971. Fascinating portrayal of psychedelic drug researcher gone Hindu.

Rodewyk, A. *Possessed by Satan.* Garden City: Doubleday, 1975. A good review of history, signs and symptoms of obsession and possession.

Rossi, R. "Psychological and Religious Counseling." *Review for Religious* 37, no. 4 (July, 1978). Further contrasts and comparisons.

Scientific American 241, no. 3 (September 1979). A superbly readable and comprehensive collection of articles on human brain function.

Setzer, J.S. "When Can I Determine When It Is God Who Speaks to Me in My Inner Experience?" *Journal of Pastoral Counseling* 12 (Fall-Winter, 1977–78). Excellent practical discernment suggestions. Includes a list of over thirty considerations.

Squire, A. *Asking the Fathers.* Wilton, Conn.: Morehouse-Barlow; New York: Paulist, 1976. A rich resource of Christian mystical insights, this work constitutes an excellent handbook for spiritual directors.

Szasz, T. *The Myth of Mental Illness.* New York: Harper & Row, 1961. A standard criticism of modern psychiatric labels and their use.

Teresa of Avila. *Interior Castle.* Several translations available. One of the great Christian mystical classics, especially relevant to modern psychology. In addition, her *Life* gives many of her perspectives on spiritual direction.

Thayer, N. "Merton and Freud: Beyond Oedipal Religion." *Journal of Pastoral Care* 35, no. 1 (March 1981). An excellent contrast of points of view, emphasizing Merton's concept of "heart."

Tulku, T. "Dream Practice." *Crystal Mirror.* Emeryville, Calif.: Dharma Publishing, 1975. An exposition of Tibetan work with dreams, including that of seeing daily life as a dream.

Ulanov, A. and B. *Religion and the Unconscious.* Philadelphia: Westminster, 1975. A strong Jungian emphasis.

Walsh, W. "Reality Therapy and Spiritual Direction." *Review for Religious* 35 (1976). Primarily comparisons.

Whitehead, J. and E. *Christian Life Patterns.* New York: Doubleday, 1979. Stages, phases, and passages.

Index